# SCUBA PHYSIOLOGICAL

Think You Know All About Scuba Medicine? Think Again!

SIMON PRIDMORE

Sandsmedia

Sandsmedia Publishing, Bali, Indonesia 80363

www.simonpridmore.com

Book Layout ©2017 Sandsmedia

Cover image by Simon Pridmore taken at Bali Scuba, Sanur.

Scuba Physiological/Simon Pridmore. 1st ed.

ISBN: 9781979164153

Created with Vellum

# TABLE OF CONTENTS

# THE EXPERTS' VIEW

"With this latest volume, Simon Pridmore makes a significant contribution to the body of practical knowledge in the science of scuba diving. If you are looking for a thorough understanding of the science of diving and how it might be impacting your safety and enjoyment of diving, this book is a must read." **Dan Orr, President, Academy of Underwater Arts & Sciences and President Emeritus, Divers Alert Network Foundation**

"Makes it easy to understand the latest discoveries in diving research. You will enjoy reading about our current understanding of what happens to our bodies when we dive." **JP Imbert: Decompression designer and technical diving pioneer**

"As a doctor with a fair history and understanding of diving medicine and diving physiology I found the book interesting. It's the sort of book I would have loved to read in my early days. Saying that, I still enjoyed it today, and there are some lovely thought-provoking ideas and questioning of current dogma. This book is well worth the read." **Dr Ian Sibley-**

**Calder, HSE Approved Medical Examiner of Divers, Occupational Health Physician**

"An enjoyable, simplified read of a complex subject, which is easy for a non-scientist to comprehend. I would consider this an essential text for every diver's shelf." **Joseph Dituri PhD (c), CDR, US Navy Saturation Diving Officer (ret)**

Part One

# SCUBA PHYSIOLOGICAL

1

# WHY SCUBA PHYSIOLOGICAL?

By: Simon Pridmore

I AM NOT A DOCTOR, NOR AM I A SCIENTIST. BUT THE PEOPLE who wrote the chapters in this book are scientists and doctors: sometimes both.

Between 2009 and 2012, a project called "PHYPODE" (Physiology of Decompression) provided opportunities for young researchers in the field of decompression research to do formal training in a number of leading research institutions all over Europe. At the end of the project, the researchers and their tutors, all renowned and established scientists and diving medicine specialists, produced summaries of their concepts and ideas, as well as the results of their cutting-edge projects.

These were then published in a book called *The Science of Diving*. I first heard of the book when my good friend and decompression expert J.P. Imbert passed me a copy.

As an experienced dive professional who reads widely, I thought I was pretty much up to speed on scuba diving physics and physiology, but, when I read the book, I realised

I was some way behind the curve. I saw that a lot of what sport diver training agencies were teaching about things like decompression sickness and narcosis were not merely misguided, sometimes they were dead wrong and disproven by recent science.

"This is a great book", I told JP.

"How come I have never come across it before?"

He shrugged his shoulders.

"I don't know. It hasn't sold very well."

I thought I knew why *The Science of Diving* had not reached a broader market. It was heavy going and seemed to be written for a more specialised readership than the general population of divers, even experienced ones. I had to make pretty heavy use of Google to get a good understanding of some of the chapters.

I contacted the original editors and offered to try and re-edit and re-format the book to make it more accessible for laymen divers who did not have PhDs, arguing that the book was deserving of a much wider audience. Fortunately, they agreed.

Here then is *The Science of Diving* in its new form, renamed as *Scuba Physiological.* Note that the chapters are independent essays written by different groups of authors. This meant that, in the original version, there was a fair bit of repetition. Some of it I edited out: but, in cases where I thought the repetition facilitated understanding, I left it in.

I have re-arranged the chapters and reworked the text so that, I hope, divers with a working knowledge of the topics can understand the concepts explained. It is still not the easiest read in the world, however, so I have added a comprehensive glossary of terms and a list of abbreviations in the back. These should help if you get stuck.

A few key points are worth mentioning at this point.

In the scuba diving world, different opinions exist concerning the topics covered in this book.

The findings in these pages, however, are not opinions. They have been acquired by the application of science, backed up by experiments.

Some readers may discover that the verdicts reached by the scientists in *Scuba Physiological* run counter to firm, long-held beliefs. This may be difficult to accept. We are all human, after all, and we all tend to be somewhat resistant to change. But, continuing to believe that something is true just because you have always thought it to be true, even when scientific evidence indicates that the contrary is true, is not a viable position to maintain.

Having said that, the research, conclusions, theories and assumptions in these chapters are not in any way the final word on the subject.

Particularly concerning decompression sickness, work continues apace and, as is so often the case, the more scientists come to know, the more they discover they don't know and even apparently solid foundations are often found to have been built on clay.

Since the chapters were written, there have been further developments in the science of diving and there will be more. The mounting evidence against the value and efficacy of deep decompression stops is a good case in point.

To reiterate, this is not my book. The book belongs to those whose names appear at the head of each chapter. Why did I get involved? Apart from feeling that the work done by the PHYPODE team should be more widely recognised and available, I thought the book might encourage divers to question and reflect.

When you find out more about what happens to our bodies when we go diving and how little is known about how and why it happens, you see how important it is to dive safely and conservatively.

In their quest to promote the sport and develop the industry, training agencies and trainers are sometimes guilty of projecting certainty rather than doubt and pretending to be omniscient. There is certainly no omniscience in this area of scientific research; debate surrounds almost every aspect of it. This book reveals far more questions than answers.

Finally, if you find a passage difficult to follow, don't give up, keep reading. Many of the really important messages in the book are revisited in several chapters and it may be that the way one group of authors describes a topic may work for you better than another.

I hope you find *Scuba Physiological* interesting and worth your while.

If you are intrigued to learn more and already have a good knowledge of diving medicine, then the original *The Science of Diving – Things Your Instructor Never Told You,* with unabridged text, diagrams and illustrations, is available in online bookstores and I highly recommend it.

Bali, Indonesia: December 2017

2

# THE SCIENCE OF DIVING: ORIGINAL INTRODUCTION

**By: Prof. Costantino Balestra, Dr. Peter Germonpre**

THE TERM DECOMPRESSION ILLNESSES (DCI) COVERS A WIDE range of conditions with a variety of signs and symptoms, all related to dissolved gas and what happens when this gas comes out of solution. Anyone who has recently been exposed to decompression and then experiences any significant bodily dysfunction must assume that the problem is DCI related until it is proven otherwise. There are obvious, acute consequences of a single, sudden decompression, but divers who decompress normally and frequently may also develop sub-acute or chronic manifestations. These may be subtle, even almost symptomless.

Some sub-clinical forms of decompression sickness (DCS) have few or no reported symptoms and may cause unnoticed changes in the bones, central nervous system and lungs. When studying the physiology of decompression, the presence or absence of symptoms may not be the most reliable indicator. In recent years, analysing decompression stress has become ever more important in the quest to understand decompression. Current research into DCS is focused on biological markers that can be detected in the blood.

Investigators are exploring the potential association between decompression stress and the presence of micro-particles in the blood. The working hypothesis is that some of these micro-particles, possibly induced by inert gas bubbles, may contribute to the inflammation that leads to DCS. This investigation goes beyond just bubbles. While bubbles in the blood certainly play a key role in the development of DCS, their presence or absence does not reliably predict DCS symptoms. Investigating this process at the molecular level may teach us a great deal more about DCS, providing insights that we hope will make prevention strategies and treatment more effective.

Modern approaches to evaluating decompression stress have considered a wide range of other factors as well as bubble counts. These include physiological changes during and after the dive, individual factors such as age and sex, and environmental factors such as temperature and altitude. Today's approach to decompression is far removed from traditional concepts of saturation and desaturation.

This book is not only for divers to learn more about modern approaches to understanding decompression. It is also designed to contribute to expanding the diving decompression knowledge of physiologists and medical personnel.

The Internet contains already a huge amount of information on DCI and DCS. So why did we feel this book was necessary? Perhaps an analogy can help explain our motivation. Recently, a cosmetics company in Japan received a complaint from a customer who had bought some soap. When the customer opened the soap box, there was no soap inside. It was empty. The company launched a lengthy investigation and then introduced a complex and expensive hi-tech packaging system with multiple checks and balances to make sure this never happened again. Meanwhile, in India, a smaller soap manufacturer received a similar complaint. What was their solution? A big industrial fan placed next to the conveyor belt carrying boxes of soap to the shipping department. Any empty boxes just blew off the belt and only the full ones continued on their journey. Our aim with this book is to be the big fan.

3

# RECREATIONAL DIVING TODAY: DECOMPRESSION HABITS AND INSIGHTS FROM DAN

**By: Costantino Balestra, Danilo Cialoni, Peter Buzzacott, Walter Hemelryck, Virginie Papadopoulou, Massimo Pieri and Alessandro Marroni**

## Development of recreational dive limits

TODAY, RECREATIONAL DIVES HAVE DEPTH AND TIME LIMITS that allow a diver to ascend to the surface at any time during a dive with an acceptably low probability of DCS. The limits are referred to as "no-stop" because, on a dive beyond the limits, divers have to stop en route to the surface to decompress. There are several models that recreational divers can use to plan decompression.

Over a hundred years ago, John Scott Haldane, a physiologist working on behalf of the British Royal Navy, ran the first experiments designed to work out ways to reduce the incidence of DCS. He used goats as subjects, rather than people, and created a set of human diving depth and timetables by extrapolating the results to fit the human circulatory system. The original tables were validated during seven dry dives in a hyperbaric chamber and 19 deep open-water dives using teams of attendants operating surface supply pumps. The tables were approved for use by the Royal Navy, published in

1908, and have formed the basis of decompression diving ever since.

Haldane's tables were based on a gas-content model, whereby five theoretical compartments of varying blood perfusion and inert gas solubility were each defined by the time it would take that compartment to half-fill with nitrogen, assuming gas uptake and release were exponential. Each "half-time" compartment was then given a maximum ratio of tolerable supersaturation before the gas would no longer be able to remain only in solution and bubbles would start to form.

Initially, Haldane assigned a single maximum ratio (2:1) for all five theoretical tissue compartments, but, subsequently, individual ratios were adapted by the US Navy and others, allowing higher maximum supersaturation ratios for faster compartments, and lower ratios for slower compartments. Later modifications allowed the supersaturation ratio to be depth-dependent and this led to the M-value concept. "Neo-Haldanean" models work well for short, shallow dives and ascents to altitude.

Subsequently, other models were developed, including some based on bubble behaviour. At least up to 2007, bubble models had not been formally validated with human trials.

Modern dive computers for sport divers often work according to a combination of different models. This is why permitted no-stop times at different depths differ widely between different brands of computer.

You can never know which of the computers is "correct" and this can be a problem when a group of divers is diving with different computers. However, because there is a psychological barrier that prevents a diver from surfacing before a computer has "cleared", in practice, divers in a group usually follow the most conservative profile.

## Dive computer validation: the problem

Dive computers have been used extensively in recreational diving for the last 25 years with a low incidence of DCS. It could therefore be argued that their use has been successful. However, there have been reported cases of DCS, even neurological DCS, on no-stop dives where divers have followed their dive computers. Indeed, DAN Europe statistics suggest that around 80% of divers who got neurological DCS did not violate the recommendations of their computer.

Not many divers realise that at the moment there is no uniform procedure for testing and validating dive computers. They are not even listed under the European Union directive for personal protective equipment (PPE Directive 89/686/EEC). The standard usually applied for CE certification of dive computers is EN13319, which is concerned only with the accuracy of the depth sensor and timer.

At the moment no dive computer manufacturer provides any information about which decompression model they use or how the model is implemented. Neither has any company ever performed any substantial human validation.

## What do we mean by validation?

To develop a validation procedure and guidelines, you have to define clearly what the purpose of a dive computer is. In addition to acting like a timer and depth/pressure sensor in real time, divers rely on dive computers to calculate remaining no-stop time at depth, or decompression stops during decompression diving.

When we acknowledge warnings in dive computer manuals or sign liability release forms to go diving, what we are doing is tacitly accepting that the probability of developing DCS is never zero. We trust our computers to help us keep the probability of developing DCS below a threshold that is personally acceptable to us. However, no dive computer can quote the probability of DCS for any specific dive plan. So we are just blindly assuming that the information our dive computer gives us has been somehow validated as generally acceptable.

The first step in devising validation procedures is to define the sort of diving for which the computer is valid. For instance, a scuba dive can mean anything from a deep commercial decompression dive in freezing water at night to a shallow recreational no-stop dive in warm clear water in the middle of the day. If you can clearly define how a dive computer will be used, you can then set precise requirements for decompression calculations and other operational needs.

Operational needs form part of the validation process as they have an impact on whether the dive computer is safe to use. Relevant factors include ease of operation, the clarity and unambiguity of the information displayed, especially in poor light; battery life; and the display and post-dive download of dive profile data.

### Decompression calculations

There are two ways to validate decompression calculations produced by a dive computer, depending on whether or not the manufacturer clearly states which diving algorithm it is using in its computers.

Where the algorithm is published and publicly known, the manufacturer does not have to prove the algorithm's validity. It just needs to show that it has been faithfully implemented. Proving the validity of the algorithm; that is, the probability of DCS when using it, is the responsibility of the algorithm's developer, who needs to show that it is suitable for the type of diving being undertaken.

Where the algorithm is not revealed, the predictions of the dive computer should be tested against relevant profiles of known DCS probability, for example, the US Navy's database of manned dives.

However, again it is important to define the type of diving the computer will be used for, so that its predictions can be compared to relevant data. As dive computers allow for "real-time" calculations and the variety of combinations is endless, a perfect validation would require an infinite number of profiles to be tested.

Obviously, this is impossible and even testing many different profiles would be time-consuming and expensive. It is also very difficult to compare computer readings with dive profiles that carry a known probability of DCS, as these are usually single, square, decompression table dives. By contrast, typical recreational dive profiles today are repetitive, multi-day, multi-level and can involve other factors such as gas switches.

When you compare dive computers' predictions and known outcomes to assess the probability of DCS, the question is, do you also include marginal DCS events and those for which diagnosis was uncertain? DCS involves a wide range of symptoms and if you cluster all cases, from major to marginal, together this may conceal the fact that different causes and mechanisms are involved.

In addition, there is the ethical issue of testing the probability of DCS on human beings, as this requires inducing DCS in a small fraction of test subjects. The incidence of DCS among recreational divers is so low that exposing test subjects to a higher risk just for validation purposes is considered unethical. Using the excellent US Navy database poses a problem because the data therein come mainly from military test subjects, who are mostly young, male, fit, well-trained, and healthy adults. They are therefore not representative of the general recreational diving population.

This is why the detection of vascular gas emboli (VGE) in the bloodstream has been proposed as a way of validating diving algorithms. It may seem obvious that the more VGE there are during decompression, the higher the risk of DCS.

However, this is not the case: the presence of VGE does not seem to be a very accurate predictor of DCS risk. On the other hand, the absence of VGE does indeed correlate with very low to non-existent DCS risk.

### Development, testing and validation proposals for dive computers

The Validation of Dive Computers Workshop (Gdansk, Poland, 2011) proposed the following procedures for validating all dive computers: -

1. Specify the principal functions of the dive computer, including display, mechanical design, performance and operational range.

2. Describe the potential risks of diver error, such as exceeding depth limit or no stop time, or dive computer malfunction. Include the severity of each risk and the probability of the risk occurring.

3. Describe, prevent and limit the consequences of dive computer failure; for example, by clearly indicating a possible malfunction and by providing minimal data display in the event of a calculation failure.

4. Design the hardware and software for the dive computer and establish verification and validation plans.

5. Check the final product against the complete list of requirements, including safety requirements.

### Insights from the DAN Europe database

In 2010, Petar J. Denoble of the Divers Alert Network (DAN) stated that:

> *"Validation of decompression safety is complicated and expensive. Thus, in most cases, manufacturers do not have the data necessary to support claims of risk control or risk reduction — an important issue for divers."*

Most recreational divers today use dive computers and trust them completely. However, the validation protocols underlying the marketing of such computers and the algorithms they use are far from perfect and even the most reliable computers still accept a probability of DCS ranging from 2 to 5%, with the probability of neurological DCS lying in the range of 0.2 - 0.5%. Most recreational divers do not know this. They tend to believe that their dive computers are infallible and that no harm will befall them if they follow them faithfully. Professionals in diving medicine and technology know that this is not the case and that DCS is always possible, albeit rare.

The DAN Europe Diving Safety Laboratory (DSL) database contains information about divers and dives in order to promote diver safety. Personal information, details of the breathing gas used, equipment malfunctions and medical history are recorded using a questionnaire. Any diver can contribute to this database. In addition, DAN Europe organises and supports field research trips, during which complete dive profiles are recorded and added to the database.

As of the end of 2013, the DSL database included the details of 2615 divers (2176 male and 439 female), who had recorded 39944 dives, (32890 male dives and 7054 female dives). 181 DCS cases were recorded giving an overall DCS prevalence of 0.45%. The true prevalence of DCS in the recreational diving population is likely to be much lower, as many of these dive profiles were collected when divers presented themselves for treatment. Also, the data mostly came from enthusiastic, frequent divers, rather than occasional divers. 91% of the dives were performed by divers carrying dive computers, mostly using Bühlmann ZHL or Wienke RGBM algorithms.

The incidence of other problems during the dives on the database is also very low. The majority of these relate to equalisation (1.24%), buoyancy (0.50%), ascent speed (0.47%) and out-of-air situations (0.45%).

### Does the algorithm matter?

Initially, the DSL database was only compatible with compartmental model dive computers, so a direct comparison of the incidence of DCS between compartmental and so-called "bubble" models was not possible. But later it became possible to collect data from virtually all recreational dive computers. Note that bubble models like Wienke's RGBM are implemented mathematically as compartmental models on dive computers, with correction factors added to account for bubble model behaviour.

In 10738 dives using Bühlmann ZHL16 or Wienke RGBM algorithms and where a full dive profile was available, 165 DCS cases were recorded. The distribution between the two types of model was 1.35% ZHL16 vs. 1.75% RGBM.

The incidence of DCS on these dives is higher than the overall incidence of DCS within the entire sample of dives collected but this is probably an overestimation due to data collection bias.

Having complete dive profiles permits the calculation of inert gas supersaturation levels for different tissues at different points in time, (i.e. M values). Interestingly, only 10% of these DCS cases involved a level of 90% or more of the M-value of the "fast" tissue compartment. Only another 10% recorded a supersaturation level of between 80 and 90% of the M-value. The remaining 80% of the DCS cases involved supersaturation levels lower than 80%, with a general average of 75%.

This suggests that there is more to decompression algorithm validation than compartment supersaturation estimates based on depth-time profiles alone. A fast ascent rate may have been the deciding factor in many of these cases, in which case moment-to-moment supersaturation, relative to the ambient pressure, may come into play.

The DAN Europe DSL database also captures other parameters that may or may not be relevant to the incidence of DCS. In time, these data may help improve decompression practice.

### VGE measurements

At the time of writing, a total of 1181 Doppler measurements have been taken on dives included in the DSL database, with 2100 more waiting to be evaluated. For dives where the complete dive profile was available, Gradient Factor (GF) calculations showed that the maximal saturation of medium half-time tissues was not reached in the vast majority (95%) of the documented dives. This was reflected by the Doppler tests, which only rarely reported high (abundant bubbling) VGE grades.

As Denoble remarked:

> *"Validation of decompression safety may be speeded up by using VGE in place of DCS as the outcome of interest. VGE may be detected in divers without DCS symptoms. When bubbles become abundant, the risk of DCS increases. Decompression trials that use VGE grade as the outcome, however, do not provide exactly the same insights as studies that include actual cases of DCS."*

### (De)hydration

Analysis of recorded DCS incidents has led to consideration of parameters other than just Doppler scores and dive profiles. The diver's state of hydration is an example.

Recent data, taken from technical divers and French Navy divers, has shown the importance of normal levels of hydration. Each group of divers did the same dive, once when they were normally hydrated and once when they were hyper-hydrated. The bubble counts, measured with echography, were much higher when the divers were only normally hydrated.

Other data from technical divers found that, even after very deep dives (down to 130 m (430ft)), no hemoconcentration (an increase in red blood cell concentration when the level of blood fluid drops, a typical sign of dehydration) was found immediately after the dive. This seems unusual since divers attending hyperbaric recompression centres for treatment of suspected DCS are usually hemo-concentrated.

A new model is required to understand this discrepancy. Perhaps the effect of immersion diuresis is countered - for a limited time - by water shifting towards the vascular compartment from the extracellular compartment. This is a good thing during off-gassing because the nitrogen gradient goes from the tissues to the vascular bed and vascular dilution is useful for handling the increased nitrogen load.

This, however, only occurs temporarily and data show that there is a reversal of the fluid shift at some point after the dive. Water moves back into the extracellular compartment, causing delayed hemoconcentration unless the diver has taken on extra fluids. If this reversal of the fluid shift occurs when the supersaturation has not yet been sufficiently reduced by the pulmonary wash-out of nitrogen, bubbles might become trapped in the dehydrated microcirculation, causing damage and clinical symptoms of DCS. This might explain why most divers presenting with DCS are found to be hemo-concentrated.

On the contrary, a minor hemo-concentration may not necessarily be a bad thing in some circumstances. A French Navy group, looking at plasma volume (plasma transports nitrogen to the tissues), hypothesised that slight dehydration at the start of the dive might lead to a reduction in the saturation rate, and thus offer a degree of protection, rather than the opposite. This has been tested using sauna exposure before diving. Of course, a sauna not only causes minor dehydration. It also has other interesting preconditioning effects, such as increased cardiovascular activity similar to that created by mild physical effort, increased Heat Shock Protein production and increased Flow Mediated Dilation. Research continues to clarify this paradox further.

## Conclusions

The data from the DAN Europe DSL Database, collected from real-life dives and situations, indicate that most recreational diving activity takes place with tissue saturation limits well within the boundaries suggested by the dive computer used, with an average supersaturation of below 80% of the 12.5-minute M-value of the Bühlmann ZHL 16 decompression algorithm.

On these dives, however, several DCS cases have been recorded, which could not have been accurately predicted by the dive computer algorithms, as they occurred with computed supersaturation levels well below the accepted maximum safe M-values. This suggests that other individual physiological factors may have been involved.

The complex physiology of decompression involves not only gas pressures and virtual compartments or other models but also highly variable physiological parameters such as body temperature, hydration state and vascular vs. extracellular fluid shifts.

Given the very low incidence of DCS, DAN believes that any major effort to improve decompression algorithms in recreational dive computers may be a costly and ultimately rather futile endeavour, unless they are directed towards a personalised decompression algorithm that takes into account individual physiological parameters.

It may be much more useful to collect more data and run more controlled experiments to find out what influence these physiological variables have and how important they are.

The objective and quantitative measurement of VGE may be a much more logical approach than tracking the incidence of DCS because it can produce results at a level lower than clinical symptoms. The aim would be to reduce decompression stress, instead of just preventing clinical DCS. As the relationship between bubbles and DCS is not straightforward, additional factors such as oxidative stress also need to be measured.

It seems the reliability limit of existing dive computer validation protocols has been reached and that the new frontier will be to further improve our ability to customise the conservatism levels in dive computers according to physiological variables.

This could be based on available scientific evidence such as the database mentioned above or by real-time sensor technology permitting a direct diver-to-dive computer interface.

As Lang and Angelini said in 2009:

> *"Any parameter that gives online feedback into a decompression model as to the state of the diver with respect to potential DCS would be a tremendous benefit."*

## Summary

Compared with other adventure sports, scuba diving remains a relatively safe activity but it is important to define the risk as precisely as possible.

Diving databases such as DAN Europe's DSL collection can record the incidence of DCS as well as provide new insights into why diving accidents take place. Data from the DSL show that dive computers are used by as many as 95% of recreational divers.

The most widely used computers run Bühlmann ZHL or Wienke RGBM-based algorithms, with a roughly 50/50 distribution of each within the DAN Europe DSL diver population.

The DSL database records the risk of DCS using either algorithm but analysis shows that the vast majority of recorded DCS cases occurred without any algorithm violation, in other words, with compartment inert gas pressures well within allowable limits. Other physiological variables may therefore be involved.

Current dive computer validation procedures, although important and useful as a first benchmark, still allow for a probability of DCS beyond ideal acceptable levels for recreational sport.

A more aggressive approach to testing and validation of decompression algorithms should be implemented to further reduce the risk. This approach could identify and control the most significant physiological variables involved in the development of DCS and relate these, along with inert gas supersaturation values, to decompression algorithms.

**Take home messages**

- Scuba diving is a relatively safe activity.
- Recreational dives are routinely carried out to approximately 80% of the supersaturation M-values.
- Validation of dive computers is difficult for typical recreational multilevel repetitive and multi-day profiles.
- Databases are especially useful because they collect supplemental data: dive profile analysis alone cannot accurately predict DCS risk.
- The reliability limit of existing dive computer validation protocols has been reached and the new frontier will be individual customisation of the conservatism levels in dive computers according to physiological variables.

4

# OVERVIEW OF DECOMPRESSION MODELS

By: Virginie Papadopoulou, Georgi Popov, Robert J. Eckersley, Costantino Balestra, Thodoris D. Karapantsios, Meng-Xing Tang, Danilo Cialoni, Jacek Kot

## Dissolved gas phase models: Haldanean-based traditional decompression theory

HALDANE IS CONSIDERED THE FATHER OF MODERN decompression theory. He suggested that different tissues of the body absorb and release nitrogen at different rates and proposed four basic principles that agreed with the observations on which he based his decompression theory.

These were:

1. Gas absorption and elimination in a tissue occur exponentially: (the Haldane model assumes that perfusion is the limiting factor).

2. Different tissues absorb and release gas at different rates.

3. Decompression is achieved by decreasing ambient pressure.

4. Gas pressure in a tissue must not exceed a level of approximately twice the ambient pressure.

He used five tissue compartments with half-times of 5, 10, 20, 40 and 75 minutes to produce the decompression calculations that led to the first practical dive tables. Haldane was also the first to notice that decompression is most dangerous near the surface because of the greater difference in pressure. This contradicted previous guidelines that allowed divers to ascend faster, the closer they came to the surface.

Haldane's perfusion-limited model was used until the 1960s without any fundamental changes apart from the addition of a slower compartment with a 120min half-time. When the US Navy started diving deeper, Haldane's 2:1 ratio was shown to be too conservative for the faster tissues, but not conservative enough for the slower ones, and the idea that each compartment should have its own allowable supersaturation ratio was introduced. As an interesting aside, the reason the first modification of the 2:1 ratio was decreased to 1.53:1 was that it was agreed that only nitrogen played a role in DCS, rather than both nitrogen and oxygen as Haldane had originally assumed.

Robert D. Workman of the US Navy Experimental Diving Unit (NEDU) revised Haldane's model to take this into account and introduced the term "M-value" to describe how much over-pressurisation each compartment could tolerate at each depth. He also added a further three tissue compartments with longer half-times of 160, 200 and 240 minutes and was the first person to present an equation that could be used to calculate the parameters for any depth. This proved to be a crucial development that would later lead to dive computers.

The M-value of each compartment is a linear relationship $M = \Delta M \times D + M0$ where M is the tolerated inert gas pressure in the hypothetical tissue compartment, ΔM is the slope of the M-value line, D is the depth pressure (gauge pressure) and M0 is the intercept at zero depth, that is, the surfacing M-value at sea level. Two practical consequences of this equation are that

1) the allowable step in decompression is greater at deeper depths and

2) a diver can surface with a degree of supersaturation post-dive (M0).

Professor Albert A. Bühlmann then extended the number of compartments to 16 and investigated the effects of diving at altitude in mountain lakes after noticing a very high incidence of decompression sickness in people who conducted dives at altitude using sea-level tables. He also developed M-values, which, like Workman's, expressed a linear relationship between ambient pressure and the maximum tolerated inert gas pressure in the compartment. The difference was that his M-values were based on absolute pressure, taking altitude into account. Bühlmann's algorithm appeared in his 1983 book "Decompression-Decompression Sickness", and it soon became the basis for most dive computer programmes.

### Silent bubbles and deep stops: redefining DCS

The traditional Haldanean approach to decompression and its Bühlmann sequel were challenged in the late 1960s when, using Doppler ultrasound, Merrill Spencer showed that divers who did not have DCS still had bubbles in their blood vessels after diving. This challenged the Haldanean models as these were based on the assumption that bubble formation only happened when an M-value was exceeded. Because the divers tested had all dived well within the limits of the decompression models and showed no signs of DCS, those bubbles were referred to as "silent" or "asymptomatic" bubbles. The discovery of their existence led to the development of new decompression models.

Typically, it was thought, silent bubbles did not interfere with the normal functions of the body and, after forming, they became trapped in the small blood vessels in the lungs and were gradually breathed out. However, if divers were doing two or more dives in close succession, the silent bubbles from one dive will still be present at the beginning of the next. Therefore, they had to be taken into account. Silent bubbles were also linked to post-dive fatigue.

In addition to this practical consideration, the existence of silent bubbles also challenged the Haldanean models on a theoretical level, as it showed that the belief that bubble formation equated to DCS and that liquids like blood would hold gas in a state of supersaturation, provided the supersaturation did not exceed a critical limit, was wrong. A new definition of how many and how big silent bubbles needed to be to cause DCS was required.

In Haldanean models, the decompression algorithm calculates what depth a diver is allowed to ascend to, so as not to exceed the M-values for the different compartments. The diver then ascends at the appropriate rate and waits for the required amount of time at that depth before ascending again to the next allowed depth. This procedure is repeated until the surface can be reached without exceeding any M-value. Theoretically, this not only ensures that the diver does not get DCS but also minimises the time spent decompressing. These are the aims of every decompression model. Haldanean models are characterised by relatively fast initial ascents.

The original Haldane model has been modified several times and these modifications included the introduction of deeper initial stops for decompression. These were shown to significantly reduce the number of silent bubbles formed. Richard Pyle introduced the idea of deep stops (also known as Pyle stops), a concept derived from his personal experience. Pyle would collect deep-water fish for the University of Hawaii and, to keep the fish alive, he had to stop on his ascent to puncture their swim bladders and let air out.

Assessing his fatigue after dives when he caught fish and dives when he didn't catch any fish, Pyle concluded that the deep bladder-puncturing stops made him less tired. His method consisted of making an additional stop between his maximum depth and his first required decompression stop, at half the distance between them if that distance was less than 9m (30ft) and at further intervals again if the distance between stops was still greater than 9m (30ft).

There is much debate today over the actual benefit of deep stops, as there is also evidence that this practice may merely shift the decompression burden further into the slower tissues, thus potentially increasing DCS risk for some dive profiles.

Pyle's empirical approach evolved into the Gradient Factors (GFs) theory, which aimed to reduce silent bubbles within the Bühlmann model.

The principle was to increase safety by staying further away from the M-values. GFs are expressed as percentages between saturation and supersaturation, i.e. a 0% GF is equivalent to the saturation line, whereas a 100% GF is the M-value line.

In practice, Gradient Factors are used in pairs, with a lower GF (Lo) value indicating the level of conservatism during the deeper part of the decompression phase and an upper GF (Hi) value for the shallower stops. These are usually set as 30% and 80% respectively.

## Tracking free-phase gas (bubbles): dual-phase models

The traditional decompression models are sometimes called "dissolved gas models", as they are based on the assumption that inert gases are held in solution in the tissues until they exceed their M-values (supersaturation) and then form bubbles, which cause decompression sickness.

As we now know, this is not necessarily the case. The presence of silent bubbles challenges this assumption and "dual-phase" bubble models were developed to take silent bubbles into account.

In the early 1970s, Australian PhD student Brian Hills developed a kinetic and thermodynamic approach to decompression sickness, tracking not only the dissolved gases in tissues but also the gas in the form of bubbles (hence "dual-phase").

His ideas were initially criticised and it was only much later that others followed his research. Among these were Val Hempleman and Tom Hennessy, who suggested the introduction of a critical limit to the total volume of free phase gas (i.e. bubbles) as a definition for DCS, and David Yount's Tiny Bubble Research Group in Hawaii, which investigated factors influencing bubble formation.

Dual-phase bubble models track both the free-phase gas and the dissolved gas phase. Like traditional models, they consider several compartments, with different half-times determining the rate of uptake into, and release out of, each compartment. Decompression is then optimised by controlling the total volume of free gas while ascending, limiting the number of bubbles and tracking their total volume.

The main assumption is the statistical distribution of bubble sizes. An example of this model is the one developed by Hills and Le Messurier, which advocates a very low level of supersaturation.

The Varying Permeability Model (VPM) is a dual-phase model with 32 compartments, 16 that track nitrogen loading, and 16 that track helium loading (for mixed gas diving). As a dual-phase model, VPM does not monitor M-values. Instead, the ascent is limited only by bubble considerations.

The assumption guiding VPM is that micronuclei, the gas seeds which are presumed to be at the origin of the formation of bubbles, are present in the body at all times, even before the dive, and even in non-divers. They are small enough so that they remain in a solution but do not get completely "crushed" under pressure: ("crushing" occurs when a small bubble is exposed to a certain overpressure). (Note that this view has recently been challenged.)

Originally, VPM based its decompression algorithm on bubble numbers, that is, no more than a certain number of bubbles should be formed. However, this was shown to be much too conservative for non-saturation diving and led to the development of a Critical Volume Algorithm that instead limits the total volume of free gas during decompression, to wit: total volume depends on Gradient x Time x Number of bubbles.

The basic assumption is that DCS only occurs above a certain threshold of free gas volume. The model was further developed into VPM-A between 1999 and 2001 by Dr David Yount, Erik Baker and Eric Maiken (Hawaii University) to incorporate repetitive diving, multiple inert gases and gas switches.

VPM-A quickly became very popular with the technical diving community as it was available free of charge via the Internet.

A fundamental flaw in the model was spotted and corrected in 2003 by Erik Baker. He noticed that VPM-A only calculated a supersaturation gradient at the start of the ascent and did not update it for every depth. His new version was called VPM-B.

In 2005 the model was made more conservative by Ross Hemingway. He developed a popular computer programme (Z-Planner / V-Planner) for calculating decompression stops, allowing a user to reduce the allowed gradients in shallow depths, to build in an additional safety margin for difficult dives. Hemingway's model was called VPM-B/E.

Bruce Wienke's Reduced Gradient Bubble Model (RGBM) claims also to consider some of the known risk factors for DCS such as water temperature, flying after diving and altitude diving, as well as reverse profile diving, repetitive diving and mixed gas diving.

RGBM is a dual-phase model and follows the logic of the VPM model. A set of "bubble factors" is used to take into account the conditions of the dive. For instance, one bubble factor is for repetitive diving over a period of hours, one is for repetitive diving over several days and another is for reverse profile diving.

Each bubble factor is then applied to the base-level gradient to adjust the decompression profile.

## Alternative models that work

Other models exist, in addition to those described above. Here are the most popular, along with their basic assumptions and the ways in which they differ from RGBM.

### RNPL - diffusion limited

All the models discussed so far have been models that assume that it is perfusion to the tissues that control the uptake of inert gas. The model developed by the Royal Naval Physiological Laboratory (RNPL) challenges this view by considering the diffusion rates of inert gas from the capillaries to the tissues. The most current version of this model is BSAC-88, which is taught to many recreational divers in the UK.

### US Navy Thalmann algorithm

Captain Ed Thalmann was the original developer of this model, commissioned by the NEDU to be incorporated into a dive computer algorithm. The main difference between this and RGBM is that, although the on-gassing of tissues is considered to be exponential, off-gassing is linear, in an effort to limit silent bubbles. In 2001, this model was incorporated into the dive computers used by Navy SEAL teams.

### Probabilistic models

There have been several attempts to incorporate a probabilistic approach into decompression models. These tend to be debated on theoretical grounds. A key point of debate is the extrapolation necessary to apply the approach to a sufficiently large sample.

A probabilistic model has been used to update and extend the US Navy's Thalmann algorithm. It calculates the probability of DCS occurrence for a particular profile from a calibration database.

Like deterministic models, probabilistic models rely heavily on decompression models and their parameters. They do not take into account different individual physiologies and fitness levels.

The general recreational diving population is much more diverse in these respects than the fit, 20-something navy divers that the models were tested on.

### DCIEM model

Developed by the Canadian Defence and Civil Institute of Environmental Medicine (DCIEM), a key difference between this and other models is that compartments are not seen as independent from each other. Instead, they diffuse to and from one another.

The current version of this model was published in 1992. It is considered one of the safest decompression table models, with over 5000 dives performed in testing. The validation process included measuring VGE.

It is interesting that, in developing these other decompression models, one of the recurrent tweaks that had to be applied was, in practice, equivalent to incorporating deeper stops. As mentioned earlier, human trials have yet to confirm if current deep-stop practices are an improvement or even, in some circumstances, an additional risk, compared to standard profiles.

For the majority of recreational and technical diving, the tables produced using these different models are very similar, despite theoretical differences. This is because the parameters of all the models have been greatly adjusted to fit observational data.

## Bubble formation and bubble growth: what is unknown

Bubbles are known to form in the body after scuba dives, even those dives made well within decompression model limits. The bubbles can sometimes trigger decompression sickness, which is why dive protocols aim to limit bubble formation and bubble growth during decompression. However, fully understanding the processes remains a challenge and several questions remain unanswered.

## The physics of things

Supersaturation can be defined as a tissue's tendency to produce bubbles and is based on the difference between the gas tension in the tissue and the ambient pressure. Supersaturation normally results from a saturated solution being subjected to thermodynamic change, which increases its concentration further, thus bringing it beyond saturation. The thermodynamic change could be brought about by an increase in temperature, a decrease in volume or a decrease in ambient pressure. In the scuba diving context, of course, pressure is the main variable. The diver's tissues take up inert gas at depth. For a diver breathing compressed air, this inert gas is nitrogen. The oxygen in the air is consumed by the cells during metabolism. During ascent, the tension of the dissolved inert gas in the tissues is greater than the corresponding partial pressure of the inert gas in the lungs, so gas diffuses out of the tissues into the blood.

"Nucleation" is the word given to the formation of a new solid, liquid or gas phase from a pre-existing phase. Here we are dealing with the formation of bubbles (a gas phase) from tissues (an assumed liquid phase).

There are two types of nucleation: heterogeneous and homogeneous. Heterogeneous nucleation is more common. Normally, bubbles nucleate from specific places, between two phases or around microscopic impurities. Homogeneous nucleation happens where nucleation does not have particular sites for bubbles to grow from. Instead, random fluctuations of the molecules in the liquid create both microscopic regions, where molecules are more closely packed together, and voids from which bubbles grow. This is not very common and usually involves a process of supercooling or superheating.

For a bubble to form spontaneously in supersaturated pure water, a level of supersaturation greater than 10MPa is required. This is the equivalent of a sudden reduction in the pressure of the saturated solution from a depth of 900m (2,950ft) to the surface. This means that bubble formation by homogeneous nucleation is impossible within the range of human decompression. So, it is unlikely that homogeneous nucleation is responsible for bubbles seen in decompressing divers.

Heterogeneous nucleation, on the other hand, can account for bubble formation in relatively low supersaturation levels such as the ones observed in the context of scuba diving. Bubbles have been observed in divers after dives as shallow as 3.6m (10ft). This has led to the concept of micronuclei acting as seeds from which bubbles can grow.

The current definition of micronuclei is small gas-filled bubbles smaller than 10 micrometres. For bubbles to grow from micronuclei, the dissolved gas from the supersaturated tissues needs to overcome the bubbles' surface tension. The smaller the bubble, the stronger the surface tension. For a given pressure gradient, there is a critical bubble size, beyond which bubbles can grow. The micronuclei theory has been around for a long time, though with little direct experimental evidence to support it.

The concept of micronuclei is not without its problems. The biggest problem is accounting for the long-term existence of these gas-filled microbubbles. As they are so tiny, they should shrink spontaneously in the absence of stabilising forces.

A stabilisation process must be present to account for their substantial half-life, a process such as surface-active coatings or a form of mechanical protection (such as the theory of "caveolae", crevices between the walls of the endothelial cells that line the blood vessels.)

Three forces act on a bubble. These are 1) the pressure of the gas in the bubble pushing outwards, 2) the ambient pressure pushing inwards and 3) the surface tension of the bubble. For a bubble to be stable these forces need to be in equilibrium. The strength of surface tension is inversely proportional to the size so this becomes the dominant force for very small bubbles. They should tend to dissolve at ambient atmospheric pressure when they are below a critical size. Micronuclei of the order of a couple of micrometres need to be stable to resist ambient atmospheric pressure. Without an additional stabilising mechanism they will dissolve immediately.

Mechanical stability is necessary for bubble stability but it is not enough on its own. For a microbubble to be stable it also needs to be thermodynamically stable: in other words, in chemical equilibrium with its surroundings. Since micronuclei are thought to exist independently of diving they should be stable at atmospheric pressure. However, without a stabilising mechanism, their surface tension would shrink them to the point where they dissolve.

There are two other possible bubble-producing mechanisms, tribonucleation and cavitation.

Tribonucleation is a term that describes the formation of new gas bubbles in a solution due to the negative pressure that momentarily ensues when two adhesive surfaces are rapidly separated from one another. This could occur, for instance, at the edge of rapidly moving heart valves.

Cavitation is the process of bubble formation in a fluid. This happens either when the pressure in a fluid drops below the saturation vapour pressure (i.e. boiling cavitation), or due to the desorption of dissolved gases (i.e. degassing cavitation), which can happen at a pressure higher than the saturation vapour pressure.

### Decompression modelling relevance

So much for the basics of bubble nucleation. The growth of bubbles is also relevant. To develop a decompression model, both nucleation and bubble growth have to be described. Combined, they enable the precise calculation of bubble size distributions with respect to dive time. This can then be checked.

In vitro physics experiments can be used to determine which parameters influence and dominate bubble number (nucleation) and size (growth). Physiological studies can only observe effects. In vitro experiments allow the study of isolated phenomena such as decoupling heat, mass transfer and gravitational and bubble competition effects.

Bubble dynamics have now been incorporated into decompression modelling, with VGE used to evaluate decompression instead of just the incidence of DCS.

## Recent advances

Via a process known as atomic force microscopy, even smaller bubbles, nanobubbles, have been observed to form spontaneously on hydrophobic surfaces. This provides a possible explanation for micronuclei, although the nanobubbles' capacity for growth is questionable. Nanobubbles are very stable but heterogeneous nucleation and tribonucleation are still the prime candidates for bubble formation in humans subjected to hyperbaric exposure.

Some new processes have been proposed that could stabilise micronuclei. Hydrophobicity of surfaces seems to be an important factor in crevice growth models and could potentially relate to physiological studies where body fat has been investigated as a risk factor.

An alternative mechanism could be that of tissue elasticity combining with tribonucleation from body movement, which could generate a constant supply of micronuclei and potentially explain some of the studies on the role of exercise in bubble formation.

In any case, incorporating bubble formation and growth mechanisms into decompression models is important and research is proceeding in this general direction in an effort to make models more biophysical and allow better extrapolation.

A consistent quantitative, unambiguous and reliable post-dive, venous bubble monitoring system needs to be developed to calibrate and verify experimental results.

We still do not know exactly where bubbles form. Bubbles have been observed both in the tissues and in the circulation. It has been shown that bubbles interact and compete for dissolved gas in order to grow. Flow conditions and perfusion rates are important factors in this competition.

There is a line of enquiry that is looking at the probability that single bubbles act as plugs blocking blood supply in small vessels. This is worthy of more careful consideration as far as DCS is concerned.

## The future of decompression theory

There is a clear need for a realistic biophysical model for bubble growth during decompression, with studies showing that extrapolation for dissolved gas models is not particularly successful. If models do not mimic bio-physiological processes sufficiently then they cannot be extrapolated to situations outside their calibration dataset. However, no satisfactory model has yet been developed.

Using VGE counts instead of only "DCS/no DCS" outcomes is potentially useful, as one study of marginal DCS events has shown. The practice of using marginal DCS events to calibrate probabilistic decompression algorithms with dive data has run into difficulty. The marginal events were traditionally assigned fractional weights, resulting in more conservative models. A study was carried out to see whether marginal events could be described instead as random incidents, in which case they should not be included. The study concluded that they should not be included, since calibration without them yielded the same results. This highlights the difficulty of looking at DCS outcome as the sole indicator for the calibration and validity of a model.

Using VGE scores is statistically stronger because the outcome scores are not binomial (yes/no), although we still do not know what the precise relationship is between VGE and DCS. Nevertheless, nowadays, the role of a decompression model is no longer simply to reduce the incidence of DCS; it also has to limit post-dive VGE counts. It remains to be seen if the idea of no longer including DCS data in model calibration, under certain conditions, would lead to an increased risk of DCS.

The current practice in post-dive VGE monitoring relies on trained observers attributing a severity grade to Doppler ultrasound video or audio recordings they get from the heart. Different scales exist (Spencer or Kisman-Masurel (KM) for sound recordings, and Ikeda or Eftedal-Brubakk (EB) for video) with 4 or 5 severity grades, but all rely on the frequency and amplitude of the signal. In other words, the number of observed bubbles per cardiac cycle as well as the relative intensity of the cardiac sound in the case of audio recordings.

However, current grading methods are inconsistent as they depend on who is doing the grading and post-dive monitoring periods vary between studies. It would be very useful to have an objective VGE scoring system and efforts are being made to come up with one. Recently a new bubble counting method on post-dive echocardiograms was shown to be more reliable than previous methods. This new method could potentially also be automated using image-processing techniques.

Modelling considerations also include finding ways to explain, physiologically, the influence of known risk factors, such as exercise and immersion, on observed bubble counts. An interesting attempt to predict the median peak bubble grade post-dive combined a dissolved gas phase model with a bubble dynamics model for perfused tissues.

The influence of exercise on bubble counts has also been investigated theoretically. Bubble formation was assumed to follow a Poisson distribution with respect to time, and bubble growth was assumed to be only dependent on pressure differences. Exercise was then factored in the form of an elevated consumption of oxygen and enhanced perfusion of tissues. Tissue bubbles lasted longer but there was less bubble growth overall. However, bubble formation could be increased through motion-induced tissue cavitation. To predict the outcome accurately, the relative rates of these processes would need to be calculated. In practice, this is very difficult.

Studies have shown that VGE counts are significantly higher after a wet dive compared with the same dive profile in a dry chamber. This is particularly important with respect to the testing of decompression models, which increasingly rely on VGE counts. If the same dive profile provokes drastically different bubble counts in wet and dry conditions, the decision as to whether to use data from dry chamber dives or wet dives is therefore crucial.

Many interconnected factors could explain the differences observed, including temperature, immersion, exercise, hydration and also the fitness of the participants. Submersion in water results in a redistribution of blood volume. In cold conditions, there is a degree of vasoconstriction in the extremities. It would be useful to conduct systematic studies looking at bubble counts in wet and dry diving, making sure other factors involved were closely matched.

### Flying after diving

A recent study on flying after diving highlighted the influence of personal factors on decompression stress. Flying after diving may increase the risk of DCS but there is no strong evidence to indicate a minimum safe pre-flight surface interval (PFSI) between diving and high-altitude exposure. The current guidelines indicate a minimum PFSI of 12 hours after a single no-decompression dive. A minimum PFSI of 18 hours is suggested after multiple dives per day or multiple days of diving, and an interval longer than 18 hours is suggested after dives requiring mandatory decompression stops.

All the above guidelines are the result of chamber trials and simulated cabin pressure conditions, but there are potentially important differences between chamber studies and field studies and the chamber trials might not have simulated all the conditions that occur during real flying after diving.

A recent DAN Europe study performed Doppler-echocardiography during real commercial flights on divers returning to their home country after seven days of repetitive diving at a tropical dive site. The results showed that with a 24-hour PFSI, the majority of the subjects did not develop bubbles during altitude exposure. However, it is intriguing to note that the subjects who showed significant levels of bubbling during the in-flight echocardiography were also those who usually developed significant levels of bubbling after diving.

It may be that inert gas accumulated after multiple multiday recreational diving may remain in the tissues of certain individuals for longer than the supposedly safe interval of 24 hours. A rapid decrease of the ambient pressure, which happens on commercial flights, may generate further tissue supersaturation that in turn, may initiate the formation of bubbles. Another explanation might be that micronuclei populations are more inter-individually varied than previously thought, and that the individuals with in-flight VGE are those who generate more gas seeds than others. Research continues to try to fully understand this phenomenon.

## Summary

Whether they use dive tables or dive computers, divers use decompression algorithms to manage the risk of developing DCS. Tables and computers dictate the time allowed at depth before the dive converts from a no-decompression stop dive into a decompression stop dive, as well as what decompression stops are needed.

These algorithms are calculations that follow the principles of a given decompression theory. Different theories exist based on very different approaches. The principles of these algorithms are very different in terms of mathematical modelling and how the modelling translates into reality.

We still do not know exactly how bubbles form and grow in the body and when they trigger DCS.

## Conclusions

In recreational diving, the risk of DCS seems to be relatively well controlled, mainly because decompression algorithms have been fitted to real DCS incidence data. Given that enough constants can be fitted to the actual data, any algorithm will end up giving roughly the same decompression profile, but this does not mean the physics and physiology modelling behind it are correct. Neither the physics of scuba diving nor the physiological changes associated with it are fully understood. Technical diving and other dives that push the limits of the algorithms carry a higher risk of DCS.

Since the risk of DCS is dependent on numerous physiological variables, research needs to focus on how individual physiological factors affect bubble number and bubble growth, so this information can be incorporated into personalised decompression algorithms.

These algorithms would take into account physiological factors and interpersonal differences including 1) personal factors like exercise, fitness, obesity, hydration, and temperature, 2) genetic factors and 3) individual responses to stress, including endothelium activation and micro-particles.

### Take Home Messages

- Following a decompression algorithm does not 100% guarantee a DCS-free dive.
- Very different theoretical approaches are used in the calculation of ascent profiles.
- Many physiological factors change during the dive and influence individual risk, but these are currently not incorporated into decompression calculations.
- More research is needed into both bubble fundamentals and bubble physiology.

5

# ARTERIAL BUBBLES, PFO AND PULMONARY SHUNTS

**By: Dennis Madden, Zeljko Dujic, Peter Germonpré**

DCS IS THE MOST FEARED COMPLICATION OF SCUBA DIVING, partly because, no matter how sophisticated your dive computer is, you can never be sure that you won't get bent. Also, it is extremely difficult to predict DCS: a dive computer can only predict statistical probability. DCS is caused by inefficient desaturation, causing bubbles of nitrogen or some other inert gas to expand in tissues or block blood vessels. Nitrogen bubbles are found frequently in the venous system after diving, but in some cases, they can also be present in the arterial system and cause specific types of DCS.

To help you understand how and why this happens, here is a quick anatomy review.

### The flow of blood through the human body

In a normal healthy person, blood is fully loaded with oxygen after it passes through the lungs. The pulmonary veins bring this oxygenated blood to the left atrium of the heart. From there, it flows to the left pumping chamber (left ventricle) through a large one-way valve, the mitral valve.

With a powerful contraction of the heart, the blood is forced through another one-way valve, the aortic valve, into the arteries. From there it rapidly reaches all the body tissues, delivering oxygen and other nutrients, such as sugar, fat, and proteins, to the cells.

As blood travels further from the heart, the arteries divide into ever-smaller branches, to eventually become microscopically small capillary vessels. "Capillary" comes from the Latin word for "hair", which refers to the fact that these blood vessels are very thin. In fact they are even finer than a hair. They measure approximately 5 to 10 micrometres in diameter.

Blood also contains other gases besides oxygen. Since almost 80% of the air we breathe is nitrogen, nitrogen is also delivered to the cells. When the pressure of nitrogen increases as a diver descends, more nitrogen is presented to the cells, causing inert gas saturation.

After passing through the capillaries, the blood begins its return trip to the heart through the veins, which are increasingly wider blood vessels. On its way out of the tissues, blood absorbs waste products from the cells: chemical substances such as lactic acid and gases such as carbon dioxide ($CO_2$). These are delivered respectively to the liver and the lungs.

### Nitrogen bubbles after decompression

When divers ascend, the pressure decreases and nitrogen emerges from the cells into the blood in the veins. This process is called desaturation. Initially, the nitrogen can be fully dissolved in the blood, but there can be circumstances where the quantity of nitrogen is too high for the gas to remain completely dissolved and bubbles form.

This process is usually compared to what happens when you open a bottle of soda. In a soda bottle, dissolved $CO_2$ is held in solution by the pressure equilibrium under the sealed bottle cap. When you remove the cap and release the pressure, the $CO_2$ comes out of solution fast and forms bubbles. Divers' nitrogen bubbles usually form because of a too-rapid decompression, but there are also a number of other physiological and individual factors that may cause bubbles to form.

These bubbles (vascular gas emboli or VGE) form mainly at the beginning of the venous circulation; in other words at the point where the gas comes out of the cells. As they become mobile, VGE are carried in the venous bloodstream towards the heart. We can detect them using ultrasound. Thanks to the work of Paul Bert in 1878, we have known about the existence of bubbles after diving for over a century.

In 1939, bubbles were found to occur even after dives conducted according to "safe" dive tables. Again, as mentioned in previous chapters, although, statistically, the presence of a large number of bubbles means there is a higher risk of developing DCS, many divers have been observed to have high or sometimes very high bubble loads without any DCS symptoms at all. This is why they are often referred to as silent bubbles.

When nitrogen bubbles form too quickly, become too large and/or too numerous, they become trapped in the venous capillaries before they can be released into the blood. They block the blood flow, preventing delivery of oxygen to the tissues and DCS occurs.

When they are smaller and fewer in number, the bubbles are carried with the venous blood towards the heart, where they arrive in the right atrium. From there they go through a one-way valve to the right ventricle, and, with the next heartbeat, they are pumped into the pulmonary artery, which is the blood vessel leading to the lungs.

Note that all blood vessels leading away from the heart are called arteries, while all blood vessels leading towards the heart are called veins.

The bubbles are swept into the lungs, where the blood vessels again gradually become smaller and smaller and end up as pulmonary capillaries. This is where respiratory gas exchange takes place. The bubbles become trapped in the pulmonary capillaries, slowly evaporate, and eventually disappear. However, sometimes bubbles can be observed in the left side of the heart which means that somehow they have bypassed this pulmonary filter.

The concept of arterial bubbles was described by Haldane in his seminal paper in 1908. He wrote:

> *"If small bubbles are carried through the lung capillaries and pass, for instance, to a slowly desaturating part of the spinal cord, they will there increase in size and produce serious blockage of circulation or direct mechanical damage."*

Haldane was writing about a massive overload of bubbles in the lung forcing their way through the pulmonary circulation. Animal studies have shown that the pulmonary filter is very efficient. However, if it has to deal with large amounts of bubbles for more than an hour, it may become overloaded and bubbles may appear in the left side of the heart. From there, they pass directly into the tissues. As about 25% of the blood pumped out of the heart goes straight into the brain, this is cause for serious concern.

Echocardiographic inspection of the heart and blood has suggested that arterial bubbles are not common during decompression. However, a very common condition called "patent foramen ovale" (PFO) may constitute a way by which bubbles can bypass the pulmonary filter. Bubbles that are visible in the arterial circulation after passing through a PFO are referred to as "paradoxical gas emboli."

**Patent foramen ovale (PFO) explained**

The foramen ovale of the heart is a remnant of the vascular system as it was before birth. A baby in its mother's womb cannot use its lungs to load oxygen into the blood. It uses the placenta instead, which brings the blood of the foetus into close contact with the mother's oxygen-carrying blood. This is much like the close contact – this time with oxygen-carrying air – which happens in the lungs, after birth.

The foetal blood from the placenta is rich in oxygen, albeit a little less rich than the blood that emerges from our lungs. A more important difference is that this oxygen-rich, placental blood enters the baby through the umbilical cord, and flows through a large vein into the right atrium. So that the blood can be sent as quickly as possible to the brain and other organs, there is a "door" between the right and left atrium, which lets through approximately 90% of the oxygenated blood.

The remaining 10% follows the normal route to the right ventricle, into the lungs, and then to the left atrium. Then it is pumped out by the left ventricle. After birth, of course, all of the baby's blood must pass through the lungs to be loaded with oxygen, because the umbilical cord has been cut and the placenta is no longer connected to the mother's circulation.

So what happens? When a baby is born, it starts crying. If it doesn't start crying spontaneously; a good slap on the butt usually helps. The baby inhales deeply, expanding its lungs fully, opening the alveoli and the pulmonary capillaries. A great suction effect ensues and most of the blood is now drawn towards the right ventricle, which by now has a much lower pressure than the left side of the heart. As there is no more blood passing through the door mentioned earlier, it fuses closed in a matter of a couple of days or weeks.

However, in about half of babies, the process takes longer. In 40% of youngsters under the age of 20, the door is still not completely fused. This door - this small, valve-like opening - is the PFO.

Normally, no blood, or only an insignificant quantity, flows through the PFO, as the blood pressure on the left side is higher than on the right side.

With advancing age, more PFOs gradually fuse closed. However, those that remain unfused seem to enlarge progressively in diameter. Autopsy studies have shown that only about 25% of people over 40 have a PFO, but the PFO is generally larger. This has also been confirmed in an echocardiographic study of divers over a seven-year interval.

### Bubbles embolising in the brain

It seems that divers who incur cerebral DCS, that is, symptoms relating to the brain, the inner ear, the eye and the upper portion of the spinal cord, more frequently have a PFO than divers who have no history of DCS or who incur other types of DCS. It is thought that bubbles passing through a PFO are quickly carried to the brain, as the brain receives most of the arterial blood.

The fact that bubbles can pass through a PFO and go straight to the brain is worrying. Some brain imaging studies indicate that even if a diver has never suffered from DCS, there are more white matter lesions in the brain if the diver has a PFO. This would suggest that silent bubbles are still causing damage to the brain, even if they don't cause any acute symptoms.

However, a subsequent, extremely well-controlled study failed to confirm this. Nevertheless, divers who have suffered cerebral DCS repeatedly have been shown to have many more of these lesions, so it is clear that having a lot of bubbles in the brain can result in permanent damage. These brain-targeting bubbles may have passed through the PFO, but they may also have broken past the pulmonary bubble filter by virtue of their sheer number.

It is not easy to detect a PFO using echocardiography. The cardiologist needs to know all the possible factors that can produce a false negative result. If they are not aware of these factors, which include proper injection of contrast fluid, straining manoeuvres and correct timing of the examination, the results can be misinterpreted and a PFO can go undetected.

## Breaking the pulmonary bubble trap

Due to recent technological advances, echocardiographs can now detect much smaller bubbles than before. Recently, using one of the new high-resolution echocardiography units, bubbles were observed in the arterial system after uneventful (in DCS terms) air and trimix dives much more often than had previously been detected by older machines. The frequency was certainly greater than what could just be ascribed to a PFO.

So if the bubbles are not passing through a PFO, they must be passing across the pulmonary filter. But how do they do this? The only conclusion is that there must be people that have connections or shunts between the venous and arterial circulation in their lungs, as it is virtually impossible to open up pulmonary capillaries themselves. A pressure of over 300mmHg, more than 10 times the normal blood pressure in the lungs, is required to do that.

Using echocardiography with contrast injection, the passage of bubbles across the lungs has been described in a variable proportion of test subjects. Percentages vary between 15 and 45%. This wide variation may be explained by the inclusion in the tests of people with undetected PFOs. However, even with reliable PFO testing beforehand, significant passage of bubbles across the lungs has been observed in approximately 10% of divers who do not have a PFO.

These shunts, or Intra Pulmonary Arterio-Venous Anastomoses (IPAVA) as they are called, have a larger diameter than the pulmonary capillaries and do not contribute to gas exchange in the lungs. Like a PFO, they allow blood and bubbles to bypass the small pulmonary capillaries that normally trap bubbles. The existence of these IPAVA has been shown using very small glass microspheres in isolated, ventilated and perfused human and baboon lungs. So we know they are not just hypothetical.

Usually, while test subjects are resting, the shunts are closed, but they open up when subjects start performing physical exercise. In almost all cases, their IPAVAs opened when they engaged in maximal exercise with maximal oxygen volume

(VO2) uptake. This may be a protective mechanism, a sort of pressure safety valve, to enable normal pulmonary blood pressure to be maintained.

The exercise intensity at which the IPAVA open up appears to vary greatly among subjects, with some individuals already experiencing a shunt when they are at rest or just engaged in very mild exercise. Other people need to be doing much higher levels of exercise before the shunt opens. Exercise or blood pressure are not the only factors. Breathing supplemental oxygen during exercise can prevent the shunts from opening. Once exercise stops, the IPAVA close again within 60 to 120 seconds.

Bubbles may be present in a diver for a period of up to two hours after surfacing. The deeper and longer the dive, usually the more bubbles there will be, although they have been observed after shallow recreational dives too. It is known that one diver may be more prone to producing bubbles than another and the factors that determine why this is the case are not yet fully understood.

If a diver exercises after diving, especially while still in the water (as there is a blood shift during whole-body immersion), the IPAVA may open and cause bubbles to pass into the arterial system. Even mild exercise like surface swimming while wearing scuba gear may be enough.

The continuous passage of bubbles into the pulmonary capillaries will gradually cause the blood pressure in the pulmonary artery to increase. It is probable, although difficult to prove, that this increase in pulmonary artery pressure alone has the same effect as exercise and may open the IPAVA. The combination of both exercise and a large number of bubbles may explain why some divers who do not have a PFO nevertheless suffer serious neurological DCS.

## Bubbles in the arterial system and decompression sickness risk

DCS occurs on average only once per 2500 to 20000 recreational dives, depending on the type of diving. However, if 25% to 40% of all divers have a PFO, and between 50% and 60% of divers have bubbles after a dive, you would expect to get many more DCS cases as, every year, millions of divers perform tens of millions of dives.

So why doesn't a PFO result in DCS more often?

In normal conditions, a PFO does not allow blood to pass from the right atrium to the left atrium. Again, it is best to visualise a PFO as a door, which is closed but not locked. Higher pressure in the left atrium keeps it closed normally but pressure from the right side of the heart can push it open. As long as the pressure on the right side is lower than the left atrium pressure, no blood or bubbles will pass through to the arterial side. This is normally the case.

However, certain things may briefly increase the pressure on the right side of the heart. A Valsalva manoeuvre, the technique most divers use to equalise pressure in their ears, is one example.

Other diving-related actions that can produce the same effect include lifting heavy dive equipment or climbing on board a boat in full equipment after a dive. Holding your breath while exerting, pushing down to pass a stool or simply coughing can also do it.

All these activities raise the pressure in the lungs for a couple of seconds and stop venous blood from entering the heart. When the activity stops, the blood that was pooled outside the thorax rushes into the heart like a tidal wave and briefly but significantly increases the blood pressure on the right side of the heart to a level higher than the pressure on the left side.

If bubbles are present after a dive they will initially follow the normal pathway and pass into and lodge in the lung capillaries, unless the diver performs one of the manoeuvres described above.

The bubble congestion that takes place there increases the pulmonary artery blood pressure and after some time, this will also increase the pressure in the right ventricle and then in the right atrium. This pressure may open a PFO and blood and bubbles will start shunting to the arterial side.

A good way to visualise this is to think of a traffic jam. Vehicle congestion creates a backwards-expanding line of stationary or slowly moving vehicles. Once the end of the queue reaches an alternative smaller and normally unused back road, more and more vehicles will start using that road instead.

Typically, DCS involving a PFO occurs about 20-30 minutes after surfacing, which corresponds roughly with the peak in the volume of bubbles in a diver. It is important to note that it is the bubbles that are the cause of DCS, not the PFO.

So the question remains. If, either via a PFO and/or via IPAVA, large numbers of bubbles can enter the arterial system, why does cerebral DCS not occur more often? Surely, these bubbles must go into the brain?

Haldane has already suggested the answer to this riddle, although it is not sure whether he was aware of it. Taking his genius into consideration, he might well have been. Let's return to the quote cited earlier in this chapter:

*"If small bubbles are carried through the lung capillaries and pass, for instance, to a slowly desaturating part of the spinal cord, they will there increase in size and produce serious blockage of circulation or direct mechanical damage."*

Theoretical bubble models have been postulated and real-life situations have shown that nitrogen bubbles that pass into and lodge in a tissue will shrink and disappear rapidly if the nitrogen pressure in the tissue is lower than the nitrogen pressure in the bubble.

Conversely, if the nitrogen pressure in the tissue is higher, then nitrogen molecules from the tissue will diffuse into the bubble and the bubble will grow, block circulation or cause direct mechanical damage.

After a dive, all body tissues desaturate, some faster than others. The brain is a very fast tissue with a half-time of approximately 12.5 minutes. This means that every 12.5 minutes, the nitrogen saturation of brain tissue halves.

So, in most cases, 20 to 30 minutes after the dive, the brain will be desaturated to the extent that any bubbles passing into it will rapidly disappear and cause no harm.

Other tissues such as inner ear fluids have slower tissue desaturation half-times and this may account for the fact that many instances of PFO-related DCS involve inner ear problems, such as dizziness and hearing loss.

The occurrence of PFO-related DCS is most probably dependent on a very precise set of circumstances: the presence of bubbles, the rate at which pulmonary artery pressure is increased and the speed of tissue desaturation. It may be that, most of the time, bubbles in the arterial system arrive in the brain circulation only after the critical time period has passed and therefore go unnoticed.

Common sense advice for divers who know they have a PFO is therefore to decrease the risk that bubbles will occur by diving more conservatively and using nitrox to reduce the percentage of nitrogen in their breathing mix, while setting their computer for air.

It is also a good idea for all divers, not only those with a PFO, to avoid straining manoeuvres or heavy physical exercise for a couple of hours after the dive, as all of us are in danger of causing our IPAVA to open up when we exert ourselves.

**Take-home messages**

- Bubbles normally form in the venous circulation and are eliminated by the lungs, but they may cross over to the arterial side.
- Although, statistically, the presence of bubbles correlates with DCS, the bubbles are usually clinically silent.
- Arterial bubbles occur more frequently than previously thought, often without acute negative effects. The long-term impact, however, is still to be determined.
- Diagnosis of a PFO should not deter someone from diving. However, it presents a potential additional risk on demanding dives.
- Exercising up to 120 minutes after surfacing may increase the risk of DCS, so all divers, not just those diagnosed with PFOs, should avoid it.

6

# DIVING AND THE BLOOD VESSELS

**By: François Guerrero, Kate Lambrechts, Alexandra Mazur, Qiong Wang, Zeljko Dujic**

SCUBA DIVING AFFECTS THE BODY IN A NUMBER OF WAYS. WE can see what happens but science still does not completely understand how and why. This chapter explains what your vascular endothelium and vascular smooth muscle are, what they do, how their function is disrupted by scuba diving and what could be causing this disruption. The chapter also examines if the effects are long-lasting, whether they can be pre-empted and what all of this has to do with DCS.

## Endothelial function

The vascular endothelium is an organ you probably do not know you have. It is a single layer of cells that completely covers the inner surface of all the blood vessels in your body.

Endothelial cells line vessels in every organ system and are strategically located between the blood circulating in your body and your various body tissues. The vascular endothelium has a significant impact on regulating your vascular tone.

Vascular tone refers to the balance of constricting and relaxing influences on the blood vessels. However, the influence of the vascular endothelium extends far beyond the control of vascular tone. It also governs the well-being of your circulation.

Normally, healthy endothelial cells maintain a relaxed vascular tone as well as low levels of oxidative stress and inflammation. They regulate the permeability of the vessel wall to plasma constituents and adequately regulate interaction with platelets, white blood cells, blood clotting factors and thrombosis.

The vascular endothelium is kept in balance by various substances that influence your blood vessels. These are referred to as endothelium-dependent relaxing factors (EDRFs) and endothelium-dependent constricting factors (EDCFs).

EDRFs include nitric oxide and prostacyclin, while the list of EDCFs includes endothelin-1 and angiotensin II. The vascular endothelium will be impaired when there is an imbalance between EDRFs and EDCFs and this may occur under several conditions. The impairment is referred to as endothelial dysfunction.

Endothelial dysfunction is associated with a number of pathological conditions, such as diabetes and atherosclerosis. In the long term, endothelial dysfunction can lead to heart disease. The health of the vascular endothelium is generally assessed by endothelium vessel dilation.

### Vascular endothelium & decompression

In 1964, Brunner and his team observed two people who had suffered hypovolemic shock following DCS. Hypovolemic shock is an emergency condition in which severe blood or fluid loss makes it impossible for the heart to pump enough blood to the body.

In both cases, the shock was attributed to fluid leaking out of blood vessels into the space between the tissue cells, something called blood extravasation. In studies of human diving, as well as animal diving simulations, DCS is commonly associated with fluid leaking from blood vessels, a condition known as increased vascular permeability.

Increased vascular permeability is caused by endothelial cells changing their form and thus losing contact with the underlying basement membrane. Severe DCS has also been shown to cause severe damage to the endothelial cells themselves. This suggests that, not only does DCS impair vascular permeability, it might have an impact on other functions of the vascular endothelium.

## Non-pathogenic decompression and endothelium

In Norway in 2005, Brubakk and his team conducted an experiment using Flow Mediated Dilation (FMD) testing after a chamber dive.

FMD testing is a common non-invasive method used to assess endothelial function in arteries. The diameter of the brachial artery is measured by high-resolution ultrasound, once before removal of a tourniquet placed on the upper or lower part of the arm, and then again after.

Following a blockage of less than five minutes, the increase in blood flow when the tourniquet is removed stimulates the production of nitric oxide in the vascular endothelium and dilates the brachial artery. As blood rushes in to restore circulation, the blood cells cause friction and stress on the endothelial cells as they rush by. The endothelial cells react by dilating the artery to handle the sudden increase in flow.

The relative increase in diameter from the baseline reading (the diameter of the artery before the process begins) is considered to be a reliable marker of endothelial health.

In Brubakk's study, healthy experienced divers performed a simulated air dive to 18m (60ft) for 80 min in a hyperbaric chamber, with decompression according to the US Navy tables. There were no clinical signs of DCS after the dive, and bubble levels assessed in the right heart and pulmonary artery remained quite low.

FMD testing post-dive revealed a decrease in the dilation capacity of the brachial artery in all divers, suggesting that even standard safe diving might induce acute sub-clinical levels of endothelial dysfunction. Later, a similar post-dive FMD decrease in the brachial artery was confirmed in divers after open sea dives using various breathing mixtures including air, nitrox, and trimix. None of the divers experienced any cardiovascular symptoms or DCS after these dives.

### The microcirculation

The microcirculation is that region in the circulatory system where gases, nutrients, hormones and waste products are exchanged between blood and the tissues. It consists of a network of blood vessels less than 100 micrometres in diameter. Adequate blood flow in these microvessels is required for normal organ function. Besides its role in oxygen supply and metabolic exchanges between blood and tissues, the microcirculation contributes to the regulation of inflammatory processes, blood pressure, and the control of tissue fluid retention.

Post-occlusive reactive hyperaemia (PORH) refers to the increased perfusion of the small arteries after a short interruption of blood flow (less than five minutes). PORH is used to assess peripheral vascular function. The technique used measures blood flow via a probe placed on the index finger.

As in FMD testing, blood flow is stopped by inflating a pressure cuff. It is then restored when the pressure cuff is released. The small blood vessels' response to the excess flow depends on the health of the arteriolar endothelium. PORH has been observed to decrease after a single air dive to 34m (113ft).

These data are in keeping with a previous study in which the authors compared the effect of multi-day repetitive air and nitrox dives on vascular function. Among the parameters investigated was the peripheral augmentation index, a complex physiological parameter related to peripheral resistance, which is the resistance of the arteries to blood flow.

The results showed increased peripheral resistance following air dives, suggesting that diving with air increases the resistance of the small blood vessels.

More recently, Laser Doppler Flowmetry has been used as an objective, non-invasive method to assess blood flow in the micro-vessels in human skin. Iontophoresis is another non-invasive method, in which small quantities of chemicals are driven into the skin in a controlled fashion, using a small electrical current.

These methods enable the precise assessment of the contraction of blood vessels due to factors related to endothelium function and other vasoreactivity mechanisms. A recent study using this approach showed that the microvascular endothelium was impaired in divers following a single open sea air dive to 30m (100ft) for 30 minutes.

## Vascular smooth muscle vs. endothelium

Vasoconstriction and vasodilatation are regulated by the action of small muscles (vascular smooth muscle or VSM) in the walls of blood vessels. These muscles react to nitric oxide produced by the endothelial cells, but may also react to nitric oxide that is not produced by the endothelium. A research group in Croatia was the first to try to assess whether the sensitivity of VSM to nitric oxide changed after a dive.

0.4 mg of nitro-glycerine was administered by oral spray to military divers after they had dived to 30m (100ft) for 30 minutes. Nitro-glycerine is used to treat coronary artery disease and chest pain by delivering nitric oxide directly into the blood, thus dilating blood vessels by directly relaxing the VSM, without any endothelium involvement. The degree of vessel dilation this induces can be assessed by echography.

In this study, the dive produced a relatively low bubble load in the divers. The degree of nitro-glycerine-induced vessel dilation of the brachial artery, measured pre-dive and post-dive, remained unchanged, even though post-dive FMD was impaired.

Lambrechts and her team assessed the effect of diving on the VSM in sports divers after a similar dive (30m (100ft) for 30 minutes on air). In this case, the average number of venous bubbles 60 minutes post-dive was 4 times higher than in the Croatian study. In these divers, the degree of vessel dilation of the brachial artery elicited by nitro-glycerine was lower post-dive than pre-dive. The difference between these results could be due to the different bubble levels or it could be a reflection of the type of divers used in the study, military divers in one; sport divers in the other.

In this study, Laser Doppler Flowmetry showed a similar reduction of skin blood flow after the dive when nitric oxide was administered by ionisation, a process whereby ions are diffused by an electric current, rather than by nitro-glycerine spray. This supports the idea that the VSM is also impaired post-dive. This was later confirmed in military divers. These studies demonstrate that alterations in vascular physiology after diving are not confined to endothelial cells alone and apply also to the VSM.

### Relationship with the number of bubbles

As decompression stress seemed to be impairing vascular function, the effect of circulating bubbles following diving was also investigated. Although bubbles are frequently detected in divers and do not necessarily cause symptoms, the bubbles still act like foreign objects and somehow exert stress on tissues.

Indeed, in one laboratory study, it was shown that cultured endothelial cells were damaged by mechanical contact with air microbubbles. Another simulated diving study showed that endothelial cells are affected during the decompression phase, even before bubbles appear. Hydrostatic pressure and oxygen both seem to play a role in this, but not nitrogen.

Going back to Brubakk's pioneering study, it found that, although there was a considerably greater decrease of FMD in divers who had bubbles compared to those who had no bubbles, the difference was not statistically significant. Decreased post-dive FMD has also been reported after breath-hold dives when no bubbles were produced at all, suggesting that post-dive vascular dysfunction does not only result from bubble injuries.

In a study by Obad, an inverse relationship between bubble formation and the reduction in FMD was reported. Following the dive, the divers with no or few bubbles showed a greater decrease in FMD than those with more bubbles. Although it appears that vessel dysfunction is unlikely to result from intravascular bubbles alone, currently there is no definitive conclusion about how bubble formation impacts vessel function.

### Duration and chronic effects

The duration of the post-dive FMD decrease was investigated, again after a single standard air dive for 30 minutes at 30m (100ft). FMD was measured at 30 minutes, 24 hours, 48 hours and 72 hours after diving, and was compared each time with the pre-dive value. In this study, bubbles reached their maximum grade 30 minutes after surfacing. Although the FMD increased gradually over time, it was still significantly decreased 48 hours after diving and it was three days before the FMD returned to its pre-dive value.

The effects of successive dives were also assessed, by FMD testing over the course of a set of six deep trimix dives (55m to 80m / 180ft to 260ft) performed over six consecutive days. FMD was measured before and after the first, third, and sixth dives. Although the decrease in FMD was similar after all dives, the pre-dive FMD progressively dropped from 8.6% before the first dive, to 6.3% before the third dive and 5.7% before the sixth dive. This suggests a cumulative and longer-lasting effect on vessel function in large arteries.

Fortunately, this effect does not appear to be permanent. In Brubakk's study, there were two groups of subjects. One group had never dived before. The second group was composed of experienced divers with an average of 726 hours of previous diving experience. Both groups were matched for age and body mass index. The pre-dive FMD in the non-diver group was not significantly different from that of the diver group, suggesting that diving has no long-term effect on FMD.

This agrees with the results of a study of French military divers who were monitored during Navy mine-clearance diver training. The three months of training included repeated open-sea dives to depths of up to 60m (200ft) with a mean number of 67 dives during the period, different breathing gas mixtures and daily jogging. There were no signs of FMD alteration after the training. This indicates that the diving-induced decrease in FMD is a transient phenomenon and, although a cumulative short-term effect may exist, there seems to be no long-term impairment of vascular function.

The chronic effects of scuba diving on skin microcirculation were also investigated by Laser Doppler Flowmetry. In this study, the effects related to the endothelium were assessed by reactive hyperaemia (PORH), while effects not involving the endothelium were evaluated by the response of blood flow to local heating of the skin to 42°C twenty-four hours after a dive.

Two groups of professional divers were compared. One was a group of mine-clearance divers who were doing about 100 dives per year to depths as great as 80m (260ft). The other group was composed of military ship divers who dived less frequently and at shallower depths, about 50 dives per year, to a maximum depth of 35m (118ft). So the divers in the second group were less used to frequent and significant decompressions.

Surprisingly, the mine-clearance divers showed greater levels of reactive hyperaemia than the ship divers. Since the response of the divers in both groups to local skin heating was the same, the conclusion was that endothelial function in micro-vessels, unlike in large arteries, is enhanced twenty-four hours after diving. In a follow-up study, when the divers were checked again three days after diving, levels of reactive hyperaemia and response to hyperthermia were back to normal pre-test levels.

Taken together, these studies suggest that microcirculatory endothelial function is impaired when measured immediately after diving, is temporarily enhanced twenty-four hours after diving, and then returns to pre-dive levels. This means that diving acts differently on microvessels than on large arteries.

## Mechanisms of post-dive vascular impairment

A variety of theories have been raised to explain the decrease in FMD after diving. One of these is that oxidative stress is involved. Oxidative stress is a state of imbalance between oxygen free radicals and antioxidant activity, through either increased production of the former and/or reduction of the latter. Oxygen free radicals are capable of destroying biomolecules through oxidation, which may lead to damage to cellular lipids, membranes, proteins and DNA.

Obad reported that the decrease in FMD induced by diving could be partially prevented by four weeks of treatment with vitamins C and E, ending three to four hours before diving, or by consuming anti-oxidants two hours before diving. There is also scientific evidence that, because of its antioxidant properties, eating dark chocolate before a dive partially prevents a decrease in FMD. This applies to both scuba and breath-hold diving.

This provides greater evidence for the involvement of oxidative stress in vascular endothelium dysfunction after a dive and supports the idea that circulating bubble formation is not the only factor in diving-induced vascular dysfunction. Obad observed a significant increase of an oxidative marker (lipid peroxidation) after deep trimix dives to depths of 55-80m (180ft to 260ft). Decreased FMD along with a detectable level of microbubbles were also noted, but there were no clinical signs of DCS.

The main molecule involved in oxidative stress is the superoxide anion, which can react with nitric oxide, leading to the deactivation of nitric oxide and the formation of peroxynitrites. Based on data showing that a) oxidative stress is increased after diving; b) nitric oxide is deactivated by the superoxide anion and; c) FMD is mainly dependent on nitric oxide activity, it was hypothesised that decreased FMD may result from the deactivation of nitric oxide induced by oxidative stress.

If this were the case, you should expect to see an increased level of peroxynitrites in the blood after diving. However, in tests, the level was either unchanged, in the case of military divers after an open sea air dive, or decreased, in recreational divers after a 34m (113ft) indoor pool dive. This indicates that this FMD decrease may not be due to the deactivation of nitric oxide.

The effect of hyperoxia on FMD during diving was also examined. FMD was not significantly altered after an 80-

minute exposure to oxygen at 1.6 Bar. This finding was confirmed by a further study, which showed no significant increase in FMD after a one-hour simulated dive with pure $O_2$ at 18 m (60ft / 2.8 Bar). However, in a study by Marinovic et al. in 2012, FMD was decreased after an open sea dive on nitrox 36 but, surprisingly, not when air was used as the breathing gas on a similar dive.

The lack of decreased FMD after air dives is surprising and contradicts earlier studies. Nevertheless, the effect of diving on FMD seems to be more pronounced with greater levels of hyperoxia.

In summary, although an increase in oxidative stress occurs during diving and is responsible for some vascular dysfunction, the questions of exactly how oxidative stress is induced during diving and how increased oxidative stress alters vascular function are still unclear.

## Inflammation

Recently, there have been reports of clinical signs of vascular inflammation after diving. Tests on graduates of the French Navy three-month mine-clearance diver training programme showed that a number of inflammatory biomarkers were increased.

One of these reports found that there was a two-fold increase in so-called "VCAM-1 positive endothelial micro-particles" after dives on air to 18m (60ft). The production of this particular type of micro-particle is an indicator of inflammation in the vascular endothelium. Significant increases were still present one hour after diving. However, no significant increase was found after hyperbaric oxygen treatment. Therefore, it is thought that the increase may be related to other factors, such as immersion or bubble formation.

Micro-particles are organs and fragments within a cell that possess their own shell. They can be found in the blood mainly after cell membrane activation and cellular destruction. In other words, they are fragments of broken cells that carry identifying markers from the original cells. By reading these markers, their origin and cell type can be determined. Most micro-particles in the blood are derived from platelets but they can also come from red blood cells, white blood cells, components of the immune system and endothelial cells.

There are substantial differences between the level of micro-particles in the blood of healthy people and the level present in patients suffering from diseases such as atherosclerosis, sepsis, diabetes, and severe chronic hypertension.

micro-particles play important roles in blood clotting, inflammation and endothelial function. It has been shown that micro-particles from patients who have had heart attacks cause endothelial dysfunction. Thus, they might contribute to the general blood vessel dysfunction commonly observed after a heart attack.

Increased numbers of micro-particles have been detected in divers after open-sea diving or dry exposure to hyperbaric pressure. These micro-particles mainly come from platelets, while the number of micro-particles from endothelial cells remains unchanged.

These post-dive micro-particles activate white blood cells and increase vascular permeability, which is the tendency of blood vessels to leak fluids into the surrounding tissue.

When strategies are applied to reduce micro-particle production, vascular changes are reduced.

This means that impairment of the vascular endothelium might be a consequence of platelet-derived micro-particles that are generated during decompression stress by their action on white blood cell activation. However, the actual mechanisms remain to be investigated.

### Endothelial function as a risk factor for VGE and DCS

The exact role of post-dive vascular dysfunction in DCS is still unclear. Diving has at least temporary effects on the vascular endothelium and the vascular wall and therefore could theoretically have an impact on the cardiovascular health of a diver, since the endothelium plays a key role in maintaining blood vessel stability. However, the fact that no long-term effects have ever been detected contradicts this theory.

The information we have now suggests that, when DCS strikes, the impairment of vascular function might just be another link in a chain that also includes oxidative stress, circulating micro-particles and white blood cell activation. In 2009 Madden and Laden hypothesised that endothelial dysfunction might occur at depth, and might therefore play a role in the initiation and the consequences of DCS. The reasoning for this hypothesis was based on the observation that improvement of endothelial function before diving helps protect a diver against DCS.

The second argument in favour of endothelial function having an influence on DCS and/or bubble formation is that blocking nitric oxide production in rats before simulated dives increases the probability of DCS, whereas administration of nitric oxide tends to prevent DCS.

Nitric oxide is also involved in bubble formation. Microbubbles are prevented by the administration of nitric oxide. Both bubble formation and DCS seem to be moderated by the presence of nitric oxide from the vascular endothelium. Therefore, a reduction in the availability of nitric oxide due to endothelial dysfunction might enhance bubble formation and the risk of DCS. However, pre-treatment with an antioxidant, which was shown to prevent the decrease of post-dive FMD, did not reduce the number of bubbles after a dive.

If nitric oxide is indeed the key player in this, strategies aimed at increasing nitric oxide production should decrease bubble formation and prevent DCS. However, there is no evidence for this. Following a shallow simulated air dive (18m (60ft) for 80 minutes), the number of microbubbles detected was not altered by pre-dive administration for four days of atorvastatin, a lipid-lowering drug known to increase nitric oxide.

Neither was bubble formation prevented by the pre-dive administration of tetrahydrobiopterin (BH4), which increases nitric oxide production in the vascular endothelium. Therefore, the effect of nitric oxide on the number of bubbles produced during a dive is still unclear.

## Conclusions

Studies of human diving, as well as animal diving simulations, suggest that the functions of the endothelium and VSM are affected during diving and this may be connected with DCS. The physiological mechanism is associated with endothelial dysfunction, increased vascular permeability, impaired endothelium-dependent blood vessel reactivity, post-dive FMD decrease and VSM impairment. No long-term effects have yet been seen.

However, just because research has not yet uncovered chronic clinical problems associated with these factors does not mean that they do not cause problems. Endothelial dysfunction may play a role in the initiation and consequences of DCS, while physical exercise, which promotes good endothelial function, may protect divers from DCS. We see that bubble formation and oxidative stress during diving play a role in post-dive blood vessel and endothelium dysfunction.

An increase in microparticle production after air diving may be related to oxidative stress and bubble formation, which, in turn, may be moderated by the presence of nitric oxide from the endothelium. Blood vessel dysfunction may be caused by micro-particles produced by white blood cell activation during DCS.

However, much more needs to be discovered about the mechanisms involved, such as how oxidative stress is induced during diving, how it alters vascular function and how bubble formation has an impact on vascular function.

## Summary

The vascular endothelium is a dynamic organ, which regulates blood vessel activity and plays a key role in maintaining blood vessel stability.

In cases of DCS, microvascular endothelial cells lose their attachment to the basement membrane and this results in the endothelium becoming more likely to leak fluid. FMD measurements have also shown the impact of diving on the vascular endothelium. Laser Doppler flowmetry and iontophoresis confirm this.

This dysfunction may be due to VSM impairment, as demonstrated by a decrease in VSM sensitivity to nitric oxide. Successive dives have a cumulative short-term effect on vascular function but there are no long-term effects. There is also evidence that impairment of microcirculatory endothelial function after diving might be preventable or restorable.

The impairment is not only due to the presence of bubbles. Changes in endothelial and cardiovascular function after diving have been found in cases where no microbubbles were produced.

Further investigation discovered that oxidative stress was involved in diving-induced FMD changes. This confirms that bubble formation is not the only factor involved.

The main molecule involved in oxidative stress is the superoxide anion, which can deactivate nitric oxide. The presence of nitric oxide in the endothelium affects bubble formation and DCS.

However, it has not been found that reduction in endothelium-derived nitric oxide is connected to diving-induced FMD changes.

It now seems likely that inflammation generated by platelet-derived microparticles during diving may cause vascular dysfunction. This might be another link in the DCS chain that also includes oxidative stress, circulating microparticles and white blood cell activation.

However, we do not yet know exactly how bubble formation and oxidative stress produced by DCS cause vascular and endothelium dysfunction and VSM impairment.

### Take-home messages

- Not only does scuba diving produce microbubbles, but it also affects the function of the vascular wall.
- The observed consequences are mainly caused by oxidative stress, but it is not clear if these represent long-term health risks.
- The relationship between vascular gas bubbles and oxidative stress is not entirely clear.
- Further knowledge of these mechanisms may help the development of procedures that will improve diving safety.

7

# BUBBLE MEASUREMENT TECHNIQUES

By: Alain Boussuges, Frauke Tillmans

Nitrogen desaturation in scuba divers leads to the production of circulating gas bubbles during decompression and over the ensuing minutes and hours, up to three hours after a dive. Guillerm and Masurel in France and Smith and Spencer in the USA pioneered the measurement of these bubbles in the 1970s using ultrasonographic techniques. Subsequently, systems of classification to assess the quantity of circulating bubbles have been developed by several research groups.

The bubble scores, ratings or scales are based on the number and frequency of bubbles in a cardiac cycle or heartbeat. Several studies have investigated the correlation between bubble rating and the probability of DCS. Although in cases when bubbles are detected, their significance is a matter for debate, all studies agree that the risk of DCS is low if there are no circulating bubbles. Bubble screening can therefore be useful as a safety indicator for validating diving profiles. A decompression profile that does not induce bubble production in a large population of divers may be considered a safe profile.

Divers often have circulating bubbles but no resulting clinical disorder. However, the aim is to reduce decompression stress as well as avoid DCS. This chapter discusses the application and limitations of various techniques used to detect and quantify circulating bubbles.

## Ultrasonographic techniques

Ultrasonographic techniques are also widely referred to as "ultrasound", "sono", "echography" or simply "echo". All these terms refer to the use of high-frequency sound waves and their echoes to locate and display organs or tissues in the human body. This is similar to SONAR devices used in submarines and the echolocation process used by whales and bats. The frequencies used in medical diagnostics, treatment and follow-up of patients are "ultra" sounds, ranging between 2 and 18MHz, far beyond the threshold of human hearing. The following techniques have proven useful for screening bubbles circulating in the body after a dive.

### Continuous Wave Doppler

The first method used to screen circulating bubbles was Continuous Wave Doppler with blind positioning of the transducer (i.e. without seeing the blood vessel over which the probe is placed). The signal is recorded as an audio file. Several sites can be explored including the pulmonary artery, subclavian vein and the lower vena cava. The pulmonary artery outflow tract is the best place to assess how many bubbles are induced by a dive, as all of the venous blood passes through there. Separate studies by Spencer and

Kisman & Masurel (KM) produced classification systems for quantifying circulating bubbles. The KM code is more complicated than the Spencer scale, as it is composed of three parameters, frequency, loudness and duration, in various combinations. You can convert between the two scales.

The problems with Continuous Wave Doppler lie in bubble detection sensitivity (it can only detect bubbles larger than a certain size) and the fact that it takes a lot of training to interpret bubble signals correctly. Therefore, results may vary according to the experience of the observer, so it is important to be cautious when interpreting statistical results, especially when comparing results produced by different observers.

### Transthoracic echocardiography (TTE)

Transthoracic echocardiography is a good tool for screening and viewing circulating bubbles in the heart chambers. Gas bubbles appear as high-intensity blobs on the images. Two-dimensional (2D) echocardiography is currently the most frequently used method for screening circulating bubbles. Images can be obtained from a parasternal view (the long and short axes of the heart) while the diver is lying on their left side and from an apical four-chamber view when the diver is lying on their back. These recordings can be made while a subject is at rest or moving or when a contraction of the quadriceps or other big muscle causes bubbles that are stuck in blood vessel walls to become dislodged and start to circulate.

In 2007, Brubakk & Eftedal proposed and validated a scoring scale, which is easily learned and executed, and recently, Germonpré and others developed and validated a new counting method whereby actual bubble signals are counted in standardised TTE image sequences.

This method averages bubble signals in the right heart cavities over 10 to 15 heartbeats, analysing only a few frames per heartbeat, just before the contraction of the right ventricle. The result is a scale that can be used to evaluate decompression stress after dives that produce medium-to-low bubble counts. Assessments of results show very high levels of agreement between observers, even those who have no medical training. Although this technique requires a rigorous fixed echocardiographic visualisation and is thus more difficult to learn than a standard 2D evaluation, it makes it possible for intelligent computer learning algorithms to count bubbles.

Preliminary tests with existing algorithms have shown levels of agreement between computer and human observers that are as high as those between human and human. This means it would now be possible to count bubbles continuously for a one to two-hour period after the dive. Integration of the bubble count is useful for evaluating both decompression stress and the effects of modified dive profiles or pre-dive interventions, (otherwise known as pre-conditioning: see the next chapter).

## Pulsed Wave Doppler detection

Circulating bubbles can also be detected using a Pulsed-Wave Doppler effect. This is based on the same technique as the Continuous Wave Doppler, but, instead of a constant signal, the probe sends out intermittent signals and records the echoes it receives back. The transducer can be positioned in a blind manner.

2D echocardiography can be used to guide the Pulsed Wave Doppler study of pulmonary artery blood flow. Circulating bubbles are shown in the flow spectrum as bright spots. An echocardiographic and Pulsed Wave Doppler bubble grade scale has been derived from the Spencer scale.

### Transoesophageal echocardiography

Transoesophageal 2D ultrasonography is a procedure in which a transducer is placed in the subject's oesophagus. The image is generally more accurate than TTE because there is not much tissue interference between the transducer and the heart. In TTE, ribs and chest muscles get in the way and the heart is much further away from the probe. However, transoesophageal imaging is uncomfortable for the subject. It is also time-consuming: medical personnel need to be on-site and the subject must not eat or drink for several hours before screening. Although it is useful in screening bubbles, in practice its use is limited to experiments with anaesthetised animals.

### Comparative studies

Some studies have compared the various techniques used for detecting circulating bubbles. Norwegian scientists found that researchers assessing subjects at rest, using the image grading system for 2D echocardiography and the Spencer code for Doppler signals, would come to the same conclusion as to the number of circulating bubbles. However, their conclusions differed considerably from one another when the screening was done on moving subjects.

In cases where the images are poor, due to movement or body composition, 2D ultrasonography and Doppler methods can be considered complementary. Reports indicate that Pulsed Wave Doppler guided by 2D imaging is better at detecting VGE compared to 2D echocardiography alone. In a comparison of Continuous Wave Doppler with blind positioning of the transducer and Pulsed Wave Doppler guided by 2D echocardiography, both methods were found to be equal in terms of sensitivity when ultrasound exploration is easy to perform and yields a good Doppler signal, for example on young athletic divers. However, in cases where the examination is more difficult to perform, 2D images guided by Pulsed Wave Doppler are more precise. Using imaging to guide Pulsed Wave Doppler helps produce good-quality recordings of the blood flow in the pulmonary artery and improves the screening procedure for circulating bubbles.

## Application of circulating bubble screening: recommendations, interest, limitations

After a dive, the desaturation process may last several hours with the maximum rate of circulating bubbles occurring 30-40 minutes after surfacing. Continuous assessments carried out every few minutes are needed to estimate the whole bubble quantity and the maximal bubble grade. Furthermore, circulating bubble grades may vary over even a very short time frame. An automated assessment method based on detecting and counting bubbles in real time would assist in analysis. Research is continuing into developing such a method. Recordings should not exceed one minute in duration in a resting diver to limit bias on the part of the subject or the examiner.

Circulating bubbles can sometimes pass into the arterial circulation via a right-to-left shunt, perhaps across the atria, via an inter-atrial connection, or across the lungs (a pulmonary shunt). Therefore, an apical four-chamber view and/or aortic blood flow recording should be routinely carried out to detect circulating bubbles in the left (arterial) cavities too.

To improve the significance of the findings, the standard protocol is to make a video file for later analysis by two independent investigators. Bubble grades provide only a semi-quantitative evaluation of the number of bubbles. For example, "Grade 2" does not necessarily show twice as many bubbles as "Grade 1" and bubbles do not appear regularly in terms of time interval and quantity. This is why a system like the Kisman Integrated Severity Score (KISS) has been proposed, where three to four measurements at various time intervals are combined into a single average measurement. These mathematical methods make statistical analysis of the data easier but they provide only an estimate of bubble production.

Since the 1980s, quite a few studies have reported a correlation between detected bubble quantity and DCS. "Maximal observed bubble grade" has also been considered as an estimate for decompression stress. The interpretations of these studies are subject to debate because correlations between high bubble grade and DCS risk are more frequently based on dry hyperbaric chamber dives and less frequently on open sea diving. Furthermore, the clinical disorders reported in the chamber are mainly articular pain or skin bends and the incidence seems to be particularly elevated in comparison with real scuba diving. Finally, as mentioned earlier, high bubble grades (bubbles throughout the cardiac cycle) are frequently observed in scuba divers without any clinical symptoms of DCS. Perhaps even more astonishing, some recordings of divers with no DCS symptoms at all still clearly show bubbles in the left heart cavities.

On the other hand, when only a few bubbles are detected during the whole desaturation period, the risk of DCS seems to be low, although not non-existent. Studies in altitude chambers have shown the limitations of interpreting circulating bubbles. For a given exposure, women formed fewer nitrogen bubbles than men but, nevertheless, seemed to have a higher incidence of altitude decompression sickness.

These observations indicate that although bubbles are commonly considered to be the trigger of DCS, some clinical manifestations of DCS are secondary to non-circulating tissue bubbles and are often related to inflammation. It is yet not completely understood which observations linked to decompression stress are caused by detectable bubbles, and which are not. Therefore, in the case of an individual diver who has symptoms, detection of circulating bubbles has no real diagnostic value.

### Conclusions

Circulating bubble detection provides a valuable tool for evaluating the safety of a dive profile in a large population. Calculating the bubble count during a whole post-dive observation period can provide an estimate of the total volume of free intravascular gas. When few bubbles are detected, the dive profile can be considered safe.

On the other hand, the value of using circulating bubble detection to assess individual decompression stress or DCS risk in small populations is debatable. As detection techniques for circulating bubbles become more technologically advanced, these conclusions may change: or they may not.

**Take home messages**

- Ultrasonic techniques allow the visualisation of bubbles in the heart and blood vessels after diving.
- After a dive, the desaturation process may last several hours with the maximum rate of circulating bubbles occurring 30 to 40 minutes after surfacing.
- Techniques to detect bubbles include Continuous Wave Doppler, Trans-thoracic Echocardiography, Pulsed Wave Doppler Detection and Transoesophageal Echocardiography.
- Counting and grading the number of bubbles after diving is a powerful tool to validate current dive tables and algorithms, assess the effect of different preconditioning techniques and therefore increase diving safety.
- There are several different counting and scoring scales to categorise the number of bubbles recorded.
- Although useful for research applications, counting bubbles has its limitations in clinical applications and is therefore of questionable diagnostic value for individual DCS risk assessment.

8

# USING PRECONDITIONING TO IMPROVE DIVING SAFETY

**By: Costantino Balestra, Jean-Eric Blatteau, Emmanuel Gempp, Miroslav Rozloznik**

BECAUSE BUBBLES OF GAS IN THE BLOODSTREAM KNOWN AS VGE are thought to be the main cause of DCS, reducing the production of VGE would seem to be a valid strategy for decreasing decompression stress and the risk of DCS. This chapter discusses six techniques that can be used to reduce the amount of VGE produced, a process commonly referred to as preconditioning.

## 1.
## Pre-dive endurance exercise

An aerobically fit diver has a lower risk of developing DCS than an unfit diver. In 1978, Lagrue and team were the first to show that subjects in good physical condition produce fewer bubbles after a dive. Studies using animals have shown that treadmill-trained rodents and pigs have a significantly reduced risk of DCS compared to unexercised animals. This effect is independent of differences in age, body fat or weight, although, interestingly, it seems the benefit of the exercise is lost after 2 days of inactivity.

Aerobically trained human runners appear to be at a lower risk for vascular bubbling than people who are mostly sedentary. Why this should be the case is not yet clear. In the past, it was thought that a bout of aerobic activity immediately before diving had exactly the opposite effect. Pre-dive exercise was seen as a factor that increased the risk of DCS because muscle contractions and tissue movement were thought to produce gas nuclei leading to increased bubble formation.

However, this theory has now been seriously challenged. Experimental studies in rats have shown that a single bout of high-intensity exercise 20 hours before a simulated dive significantly decreases bubble formation and reduces mortality. A human study has supported these data. In this research, conducted dry in a hyperbaric chamber, divers produced fewer vascular gas bubbles when they had performed a single bout of aerobic exercise 24 hours before a dive.

In two further studies, it was shown that a single running session of 45 minutes at 60-80% of the subject's maximum heart rate performed two hours before a dive in a hyperbaric chamber also led to decreased bubble production. In these studies, divers were compressed at 30m (100ft) for 30 minutes. Circulating vascular gas bubbles were measured by Doppler testing at periods of 30, 60, and 90 minutes after the dive.

Another study tested the effect of cycling for 45 minutes, two hours before an open-water dive. The results confirmed the data obtained in the chamber and found that both moderate and strenuous exercise reduced VGE production. In addition, a study by Madden and team in 2014 showed that repetitive high-intensity anaerobic exercise not only reduced post-dive VGE, it also produced lower microparticle counts. A further study showed that running on a treadmill for 45 minutes, one hour before a dive, also significantly reduced the bubble count. Nobody knows yet what the optimal timescale is for doing pre-dive exercise, or even if there is one.

It is not clear why pre-dive exercise should have this effect. Initially, it was thought that the influence of nitric oxide on the vascular endothelium might be a factor. We know that nitric oxide synthase activity increases immediately following 45 minutes of exercise and we also know that nitric oxide administered immediately before a dive reduces bubble formation. Since nitric oxide causes the blood vessels to dilate, it is possible that this helps the body eliminate gas nuclei before they turn into bubbles. However, this theory is not completely convincing. Experiments on rats have shown that blocking the supply of nitric oxide increases bubble production in sedentary subjects but not in exercised subjects.

So the effect of pre-dive exercise on bubble production may well be due to other factors. These may be biochemical processes or physical concepts such as exercise increasing turbulence in the flow of blood. It has also been proposed that pre-dive exercise may alter blood perfusion in the tissues. The uptake or release of inert gas by a particular tissue depends on both the rate of blood flow to the tissue and the rate of gas diffusion from the blood into that tissue. It has been observed that pre-dive exercise provokes a decrease in the volume of blood and thus the volume ejected with each heartbeat, reducing blood flow to various tissues. This could reduce inert gas uptake during the dive and lead to a reduction in post-dive bubble formation.

Hydration during or immediately following exercise seems to enhance the beneficial effects of exercise on decompression. Reduced bubble production not only correlates with dehydration by sweating but also with the volume of water taken on after exercise. This is consistent with other findings that pre-dive oral hydration decreases the number of bubbles in the circulation post-dive.

Taking on fluids may prevent the fluid loss induced by diving, which would result in increased elimination of inert gas during decompression. Therefore, while moderate dehydration may be beneficial at the start of the dive, it is important to hydrate during decompression, both on ascent and post-dive.

To sum up, divers should keep physically fit. Recent data strongly suggest that a single session of aerobic exercise a few hours before diving reduces bubble formation and the risk of DCS. This is probably because of two factors, one associated with nitric oxide, and the other related to mechanical stimulation.

## 2.
## Pre-dive hydration

Experiments using animals to investigate whether there is a relationship between fluid balance and DCS risk have produced limited and conflicting data.

Studies using pigs have shown that pre-dive hydration does not diminish the risk of neurological DCS and that dehydration is not associated with an increased risk of DCS.

However, in another experiment using rabbits, dehydration and the resultant decrease in blood plasma volume appeared to be a major factor causing spinal cord injury during rapid decompression.

And yet another trial demonstrated that normally hydrated pigs had a lower risk of severe DCS than pigs which were deprived of fluids and administered diuretics.

Pre-dive dehydration thickens the blood and leads to hemoconcentration. As mentioned earlier, this refers to the increase in red blood cell concentration that occurs when the level of blood fluid drops. Hemoconcentration makes it harder for bubbles that form in the bloodstream to be released. This suggests that dehydration could be a factor causing DCS.

When we dive, we experience changes in fluid distribution, the so-called "central blood shift". Because the pressure around us is increased, blood shifts to the blood vessels in the body's core, rather than the arms and legs. These changes lead to diuresis, reduction of blood plasma volume and, possibly, dehydration. Experiments have shown, however, that divers who display symptoms of DCS at the end of a dive are not yet hemoconcentrated: but by the time they turn up at the hyperbaric chamber for treatment, they ARE found to be hemoconcentrated. The hemoconcentration only occurs around 20 minutes after surfacing. It is believed that this is because, during the dive, fluid shifts from the cells to the blood vessels to compensate for the loss of fluid in the blood. After the dive, the fluid shifts back into the cells.

Post-dive dehydration and the consequent hemoconcentration could promote the development of DCS by reducing the rate of tissue-to-blood perfusion and thereby impeding the elimination of inert gas. A study of professional divers found loss of bodily fluids correlated with bubble count, as measured approximately one hour after a dive. This suggests that it is particularly important to rehydrate after a dive, especially if you are doing more than one dive a day.

A recent experiment involving military divers investigated the benefits of hydrating before the dive to reduce dehydration during the dive and prevent a reduction in blood volume (hypovolemia) post-dive. The experiment showed that drinking a saline-glucose beverage before diving significantly decreased the amount of VGE in a diver's circulation after the dive.

Theoretical models suggest that the surface tension of the fluid affects the growth and stability of a gas bubble. If surface tension is low, a bubble is more likely to form. However, in the study involving military divers mentioned earlier, hydration did not affect plasma surface tension. Moreover, there is evidence that serum surface tension in healthy individuals varies over time, suggesting that an individual's tendency to develop vascular bubbles after decompression could vary too. Clearly, further research and analysis are necessary.

Drinking water before a dive is an easy way to reduce the risk of DCS. When you are well hydrated, you minimise the negative effects associated with post-dive hypovolemia. The best way to stay well-hydrated is to drink before you get thirsty, a little at a time, say a cup of water every 15-20 minutes. Drinking a large amount of water too fast will increase diuresis, and will not hydrate your tissues.

### 3.
### Pre-dive oxygen breathing

Oxygen breathing has been extensively investigated as a way of reducing DCS risk before altitude decompression or spacewalks. Oxygen breathing is also routinely employed during decompression from deep air dives to accelerate the washout of nitrogen from the tissues, thus both shortening the decompression time and lowering the incidence of DCS. Several studies using animals have shown that exposure to hyperbaric oxygen before a dive in a hyperbaric chamber appears to help prevent DCS and reduce the generation of VGE.

This might be due to the physical effects of breathing gas without nitrogen (de-nitrogenation) although there are no data that suggest this. It might be because of the antioxidant and anti-inflammatory properties of hyperbaric oxygen itself. One study showed that using hyperbaric oxygen before a dive reduced platelet activity after the dive. Additionally, there is a theory that exposure to hyperbaric oxygen at the beginning of a dive could result in oxygen replacing inert gas in the gas nuclei where bubbles begin.

Some studies have demonstrated that pre-exposure of various organs, for example, the heart, lungs, brain or spinal cord, to hyperbaric oxygen can protect against subsequent acute ischemia or oxidative injury. The molecular mechanisms underlying this remain poorly understood but may involve nitric oxide formation or an increase in antioxidant enzymes.

In 2009, a study examined what effect breathing oxygen at ambient pressure for 30 minutes before a dive would have on post-dive bubble formation.

The divers participating in the experiment stopped breathing oxygen 15 minutes before the dive. They then did two dives, 100 minutes apart, to 30m (100ft) for 30 minutes with a 6-minute stop at 3m (10ft) on each dive.

The divers were randomly assigned to one of four profiles: "air-air" (the control profile), "$O_2$-$O_2$", "$O_2$-air" and "air-$O_2$" where "$O_2$" was a dive with oxygen pre-breathing and "air" was a dive without oxygen pre-breathing.

The study found that oxygen pre-breathing resulted in a significant reduction in decompression-induced bubble formation, regardless of the profile. The beneficial effect of pre-dive oxygen was observed after the first dive and was maintained after the second dive even when oxygen pre-breathing did not precede the second dive.

The "$O_2$-$O_2$" profile resulted in the greatest reduction in bubble scores measured after the second dive. The results indicated that the beneficial effects were cumulative and long-lasting.

The mechanism involved in this process may be based on the ability of oxygen to replace nitrogen in the gas nuclei by diffusion. Another possibility is that oxygen administration induces prolonged effects such as decreases in heart rate and cardiac output and increased resistance to blood flow. This results in a smaller inert gas load in peripheral tissues during diving and therefore a reduction in post-dive bubble formation.

These ideas have been partially confirmed in a recent study with scuba divers comparing the effect of 1) pre-dive oxygen breathing on the surface, 2) pre-dive air-breathing and 3) in-water (hyperbaric) oxygen pre-breathing at 6m (20ft) and 12m (40ft). Bubble formation after decompression was significantly reduced after pre-breathing oxygen, with a more significant reduction after hyperbaric oxygen pre-breathing.

The difference between surface and hyperbaric oxygen pre-breathing was related to the increased oxygen content in plasma and body tissues during hyperbaric exposure, resulting in a more efficient nitrogen wash-out from gas nuclei, particularly in fast tissue compartments.

Another way oxygen can be used to prevent the risk of DCS is to breathe oxygen after surfacing in an attempt to shrink decompression-induced bubbles more rapidly. Although clinical data are lacking, this procedure, termed "surface interval oxygen", is usually practised between repetitive dives to achieve some dive time extension for the second dive or to reduce the risk of decompression injury following caisson work.

An experiment with pigs demonstrated that breathing oxygen for 100 minutes at the surface, beginning twenty minutes after a chamber dive to 5 ATA for forty minutes, eliminated vascular bubbles from the pulmonary artery faster than when there was no exposure to oxygen. In humans, this has been anecdotally observed in victims of DCS where fifteen minutes of breathing oxygen has both reduced VGE and also decreased the symptoms of DCS. Oxygen is the primary emergency first aid therapy for DCS victims.

Another series of experimental animal studies also focussed on the relative importance of pressure and oxygen on bubble elimination. In an air environment, the application of 2 ATA of pressure significantly decreased the length of time required for vascular bubbles to be eliminated. However, increasing the pressure to 4 ATA and using nitrox 50 produced no further improvement. This suggests that pressure is the main factor.

An experiment involving military divers compared the effect on VGE formation of surface oxygen breathing and in-water (hyperbaric) oxygen breathing following an open-water air dive. It was shown that bubble counts were dramatically reduced with post-dive oxygen and that hyperbaric oxygen was more effective for removing VGE than surface oxygen.

As an interesting side note, breathing oxygen has been shown to increase the capture and transport of proteins by the lymphatic system. Oxygen breathing may therefore also increase the release of microbubbles from the bloodstream into the lymphatic bed of soft tissues as microbubbles have the same characteristics as large proteins. So, removing gas nuclei from the blood vessel wall may be the mechanism by which breathing oxygen reduces post-dive VGE production.

In summary, oxygen breathing before or after diving, whether on the surface or underwater, could be a useful strategy to reduce bubble formation and DCS risk.

## 4.
## Pre-dive heat exposure

A study was conducted to determine what effect pre-dive heat exposure in a sauna would have on bubble formation after a dive. Sixteen divers underwent a 30-minute infrared dry sauna session, followed one hour later by a dry chamber dive to 4 ATA for 25 minutes. Test results showed that the sauna exposure significantly decreased circulating bubbles after the dive.

Another experiment involving a group of divers who were known normally to produce particularly large numbers of VGE after diving also revealed a significant decrease in post-dive bubbling. In this study, the divers first performed three control dives in a 34m (113ft) deep swimming pool with no preconditioning. Then, more dives were carried out with various preconditioning procedures and the post-dive bubble counts compared. Flow-mediated dilation testing was also used to analyse the link between nitric oxide production and post-dive bubble count. The first preconditioning procedure involved a 30-minute infrared sauna session two hours before the dive. This led to a significant reduction in post-dive bubbles.

So it seems heat stress may give some degree of protection against bubble-induced injury from decompression. This mechanism could be related to biochemical processes involving Heat Shock Proteins. These are proteins that contribute to increased cell survival after stress.

Heat Shock Proteins are known to interact with the endothelial nitric oxide pathway, which may influence levels of bubble formation. Also, high environmental temperatures lead to sweating and this, in turn, results in dehydration. As mentioned earlier, moderate dehydration induced by pre-dive exercise also reduces vascular bubble formation. There may be a link.

## 5.
## Pre-dive vibration

In the old days, combat divers and commercial divers would drive their boat fast out to the dive site, but return to shore slowly post dive believing that this strategy would reduce the risk of DCS. On hearing this, researchers decided to see if science could back up the theory and found that 30 minutes of whole-body vibration before a dive could indeed reduce the number of bubbles produced after a dive.

There are several possible explanations. First, the vibration of a boat travelling at speed could induce changes in blood flow as well as in the endothelium, resulting in the elimination of gas nuclei. The vibration may increase friction between the blood and the endothelium, causing the nuclei to become detached from the artery wall.

Second, it is possible that vibration could increase lymphatic circulation, thus removing some gas nuclei in intracellular tissues.

## 6.
## Biochemical preconditioning

Several studies on both animal and human subjects have shown that hyperbaric exposure results in endothelial dysfunction. Endothelial dysfunction is characterised by an impairment of nitric oxide production and nitric oxide normally plays a key role in the regulation of vascular tone.

It has been suggested that endothelial dysfunction may be the result of oxidative stress resulting from hyperoxia during diving and recent experiments have shown that taking antioxidants before diving can reduce the negative effects that diving has on endothelial function. Preconditioning by taking vitamin C could reduce endothelial inflammation at depth and thus limit gas bubble formation.

Drugs known as statins lower blood cholesterol levels and are known to be beneficial in the prevention of coronary heart disease and stroke. The mechanisms of this are complex but some experts argue that statins could help preserve endothelial integrity during diving and consequently reduce bubble formation. Having said this, several studies have failed to support this theory.

Recently, a Belgian group studied the effects of dark chocolate on VGE production and endothelial impairment associated with diving and found that consumption of dark chocolate had a positive effect on the endothelium, but no significant effect on VGE production.

Other recent studies have discovered that eating 30 grams of dark chocolate two hours before a breath-hold dive can prevent the endothelial dysfunction that is normally observed in free diving. The flavonoids in dark chocolate seem to be the key ingredients. They generate nitric oxide secretion and decrease platelet adhesion two hours after ingestion and this helps prevent bubble stability.

The timing is critical. The decrease in platelet adhesion peaks two hours after chocolate consumption.

## Conclusions

VGE production is not directly related to the preservation of endothelial function. Neither is it directly related to nitric oxide. However, preservation of endothelial function after diving may reduce the adverse effects of VGE.

Some preconditioning strategies reduce VGE production, some reduce endothelial decompression stress and some have a positive impact on both. Further research is required to investigate the mechanisms underlying these effects.

## Take-home messages

- Divers should stay in good physical shape and maintain cardiovascular fitness.
- Certain pre-dive procedures can help reduce decompression stress.

- Pre-dive oral hydration, exposure to heat, whole body vibration and oxygen breathing may represent easy means of reducing DCS risk.
- Some preconditioning procedures help maintain endothelial function. Others are better at reducing VGE production.

9

# DCS EVALUATION: CLUSTER ANALYSIS OF DCS

By: Tamer Ozyigit, Murat S. Egi

DCS MANIFESTS ITSELF IN VARIOUS FORMS. DIFFERENT ORGANS and body functions can be affected by free inert gas in the tissues and circulation. This can result in complex presentations of the disease, from mild to severe. The treatment of DCS is currently based on recompression therapy in hyperbaric chambers. The pressure/time combination of the treatment is partly dependent on the type of DCS.

In remote areas such as oil and gas platforms, diver medical technicians begin recompression treatment immediately. After evaluating the type of DCS according to the observed signs and symptoms, standard recompression procedures such as US Navy treatment tables are applied.

Classification of DCS helps technicians choose the most appropriate treatment table to apply. Ways of classifying DCS are based on expert opinion and experience. Some of these methods try to create a link with the pathophysiology of the DCS. However, there are also other ways.

Cluster analysis is the generic name given to a wide variety of procedures and is a good method for classifying DCS by using statistics. Clustering starts with a data set containing information about a collection of objects and attempts to reorganize these objects into relatively homogenous groups. In DCS analysis, the aim is to group patients according to their observed signs and symptoms.

## Data mining

Modern data mining is the result of the natural evolution of information technology. Progress in digital data acquisition and storage technology has resulted in the growth of huge databases. This has occurred in all areas of human endeavour, from the common, like supermarket transaction data, credit card usage records or telephone call details, to the more exotic, such as molecular databases and medical records.

As a result, interest has grown in processing data to extract information of value. This is data mining: extracting knowledge from large amounts of data. The term is actually a misnomer. Extracting gold from rocks or sand is referred to as gold mining rather than rock or sand mining, so data mining should really be called "knowledge mining". But it isn't.

The following are the most common data mining tasks.

***Description:*** that is, trying to find ways to describe patterns and trends lying within data. This can be done by techniques such as finding averages or using graphical presentations.

***Clustering and classifying:*** as mentioned earlier, clustering refers to the grouping of records, observations or cases into classes of similar objects. Classifying on the other hand is giving names to these groups of similar objects according to their principal common attributes.

***Estimation:*** estimation is similar to classification except that the target is to estimate a numerical value for something rather than give something a name. For example, you might want to estimate the blood pressure reading of a hospital patient based on the patient's age, gender and body mass index.

***Prediction:*** prediction is similar to classifying and estimation except that the results lie in the future. For example, a stock-broker may be interested in predicting how much a stock will be worth in three months time.

Today, thanks to DAN's large databases, we now have enough data to implement data mining techniques for the classification of DCS.

## Classification

One of the main purposes of data mining is to classify objects in a database. Classification is the act of distributing these objects into classes or categories.

You can compare it to the way a language works. A language is made up of words that help us to recognise and discuss different events, objects and beings. We use nouns to describe classes of objects that have similar important features. For example, animals are given names like cat, dog or horse and these names allow them to be collected into groups. Classifying and naming are the same thing.

Classification is essential for science. Biology is an obvious example. It was Aristotle who carried out the first known scientific study for biological classification when he developed a system for classifying animals.

He divided the animal kingdom into two groups: those that have red blood and those that do not. This corresponds roughly with the more recent classification of vertebrate and invertebrate animals.

Classification has also played an essential role in the development of theories in other sciences. For example, the classification of elements in the periodic table played a crucial role in understanding the structure of the atom.

Today, academics and market researchers often need to classify people, firms, products or behaviours to achieve their goals. Organizations will process large amounts of data in order to reach decisions. Strategies used to identify population groups, such as segmentation and target marketing, would not be possible without objective classification.

The general objectives of classification are:

- 1. to understand a complex system by dividing it into classes;
- 2. to develop theoretical ideas about the characteristics of members of these classes; and
- 3. to develop general strategies for members of these classes.

Classification is also very important in medicine. It is useful to:

- 1. Diagnose disease;
- 2. Treat specific types of disease; and
- 3. Get an idea of treatment costs and duration in advance.

## Cluster analysis

A "cluster" is a group of relatively homogeneous objects or observations and cluster analysis is an exploratory tool for organising observed data into meaningful groups.

Cluster analysis creates new groups without any prior knowledge of what clusters may be formed and does not explain why the clusters exist. As a result, each cluster describes, in terms of the data collected, the class to which its members belong. Items in each cluster are similar in some ways to each other and dissimilar to those in other clusters.

The task is simple when there is a single attribute by which objects are clustered. For example, people can be clustered as male and female without the need for any complex algorithm. The primary objective of cluster analysis is to define the structure of the data by placing the most similar observations into groups. As the number of variables increases, the analysis becomes more complicated.

To perform clustering, we have to ask three basic questions.

***How do we measure similarity?*** There are several ways to compare similar objects. These include correlation and distance.

***How do we form clusters?*** Once similarities have been calculated and defined by a number then the most similar observations are collected into groups. There are different ways of doing this. For example, you could assume that every observation is a separate group and then try to merge the groups according to the distance between them or you could start with one single group and then partition it into smaller groups.

***How many groups do we form?*** The number of clusters can range from just one to the total number of observations, (where each observation would form its own cluster). The similarity of clusters can be measured. The measure is smallest when each observation forms a separate cluster and largest when all observations are grouped into a single cluster. Usually, the optimum number of clusters is determined by experts.

You can calculate the similarities between observations by using a formula. Then you group the observations. An easy way of doing this is to identify the most similar observations not already in the same cluster and combine the clusters.

Start with each observation in its own cluster and then combine two clusters at a time until all observations are in a single cluster. This is termed a hierarchical procedure. New clusters are formed by combining existing clusters, so the process can also be termed agglomerative.

## DCS classification

Classifying different types of a disease into groups is not a new concept. It dates back to the beginning of medical science. However, the application of statistical clustering and classification techniques to the medical field IS relatively recent.

As explained earlier, classification of DCS is necessary, as the ability to apply the right treatment procedure not only helps patients recover more quickly, but it also reduces treatment costs and time.

Existing DCS classifications are based on expert opinion. Writing about compressed air workers in 1960, Golding and his team classified DCS as "Type I," referring to cases exhibiting pain only, and "Type II" for cases characterised by neurological manifestations, abnormal physical signs and pain.

A third classification was defined as Arterial Gas Embolism (AGE), which referred to essentially neurological manifestations resulting from pulmonary overpressure. The US Navy uses this system of classification as a guide to diagnosis and treatment.

In Russia, on the other hand, the three types of decompression sickness recognised are:

1. Basic symptoms of minor sickness: pains in the joints, bones and muscles, skin itching and colouration.

2. Mid-degree decompression sickness characterised by pains in the bone joints and muscles and obstruction of the cardiovascular and respiratory systems. Also, cases where joint movements are restricted and painful and joint function is impaired.

3. Severe decompression sickness characterised by significant impairment of the nervous system.

Buch and his team divided the signs and symptoms of DCS into three categories: “mild”, “moderate” and “severe”.

Benton and Glover suggested seven categories of DCS: limb pain, neurological, vestibular, cardiopulmonary, cutaneous, lymphatic and constitutional.

The Perceived Severity Index published in 2002 by DAN divides DCS into 6 hierarchical groups. These are:

a) serious neurological,

b) cardiopulmonary,

c) mild neurological,

d) pain,

e) lymphatic or skin and

f) constitutional or non-specific.

The use of statistical techniques for DCS classification is very rare. Ozyigit performed a two-step cluster analysis using the diving injury database maintained by DAN America and reports from participating hyperbaric facilities, using a standardised Diving Incident Report Form.

There were 1,929 cases of DCS between 1999 and 2003, involving 1,368 male and 561 female divers. The average age was 38 with a range of 13 to 73.

Twenty-five different manifestations were reported that may have been caused by decompression and these were interpreted as DCS. For Ozyigit's study, DCS was classified into four clusters and the hierarchical ordering was similar to the Perceived Severity Index. The severity of the principal manifestations increased from cluster 1 through cluster 4.

Cluster 1 (pain only) was the least severe.

Cluster 2 represented local neurological or mild spinal involvement.

Cluster 3 represented serious spinal involvement: and

Cluster 4 represented cerebral or cardiopulmonary problems that might require urgent and aggressive intervention.

## Conclusions

Investigating different types of DCS using Cluster Analysis helps doctors with their diagnosis. Patient clusters enable researchers to analyse sign and symptom patterns in each cluster and generate rules for placing a DCS case into a specific category. This could be valuable in assisting with diagnosis in remote locations. For example, a diver medical technician could compare observed signs and symptoms to a list, then search online for the type of DCS and the recommended treatment.

Patient clusters can assist studies into the mechanisms of DCS by observing relationships between signs and symptoms in the clusters. Also, investigating the efficiency of different treatment strategies for different patient groups is useful for evaluating existing methods and developing newer, more efficient ones. Clustering patients can help estimate treatment duration, cost and results as well.

### Take-home messages

- DCS manifests itself in various forms and determining the type of DCS is useful for applying an effective treatment policy.
- The best-known classification system is AGE, Type I DCS, and Type II DCS. However, other classifications have been proposed, such as mild, moderate, and severe or the Perceived Severity Index.
- Using computer technology, large amounts of DCS injury data can be collected. Data mining techniques are valuable for analysing large databases.
- Cluster Analysis is an appropriate technique for classifying DCS and providing experts with an objective point of view.

10

# CONTROVERSIES AND REMOTE MANAGEMENT OF DCS

By: Peter Germonpre, Adel Taher, Ahmed Sakr, Guy Thomas, Francois Burman, Alessandro Marroni, Jacek Kot, Yurii Tkachenko

THE PHYSIOLOGY AND PATHOLOGY OF DECOMPRESSION HAVE been studied for over 100 years and the procedures that have been developed for preventing and treating DCS have proven to be relatively effective.

A large number of individual factors, many insufficiently understood, seem to play a role.

Even if current decompression procedures seem to work well in most circumstances, we still do not know why DCS sometimes occurs despite a diver having followed all the rules.

A considerable number of cases of decompression sickness are still classified as "unearned".

The unpredictable nature of DCS means that, to prevent it, a diver must be knowledgeable, alert and prepared. However, individual and environmental related factors can make prevention difficult.

This chapter discusses some of these factors and comes up with possible solutions and workarounds.

## Why DCS Happens

To begin, let's revisit a little history. In the 19th Century, DCS was known primarily from tunnel and bridge building, where construction crews worked at depths of 20m to 30m (66ft to 100ft) in a "caisson", a sort of upturned metal container, the open side of which was placed on the seabed and pressurised with air to the same pressure as the surrounding water.

This kept out most of the water.

After decompressing following a shift of between 6 and 8 hours, workers often complained of joint pain. They also sometimes reported neurologic symptoms and respiratory difficulties or went into cardiovascular shock. At one time, over 10% of caisson workers were reported to have experienced "caisson disease" and a significant number died from it.

It was observed that the more slowly the workers were decompressed, the less likely it was they would get the disease. Tunnel workers often had to walk for a long distance to come out of the tunnel shaft and pass several airlocks along the way, each of which decreased the ambient pressure. These were the first decompression stops.

Divers usually worked short shifts because they got tired quickly. This was because their underwater apparatus (hard hat and diving suit with lead shoes) was very heavy and also because water offers much greater resistance to movement than air.

DCS symptoms had been noticed earlier in divers working to salvage shipwrecks but these symptoms were attributed to rheumatism caused by long immersion. After a shift, divers were just winched up or made their own way out of the water as normal. Nobody thought then that such symptoms could be avoided by the divers surfacing more slowly.

For the caisson workers (and, as they would later find, for the divers), the problem was to find a way of preventing decompression problems while still exiting from the pressurised environment as quickly as possible.

Haldane proposed a practical solution in his report in the Journal of Hygiene in 1908. This is now considered to be the seminal paper on practical decompression physiology. Based on experiments conducted in a hyperbaric chamber, using goats as test subjects, Haldane came up with an allowable pressure reduction ratio of 2:1: meaning that absolute pressure (not depth or gauge pressure) could be halved in one single step without significant health problems.

Haldane also found that inert gases penetrate some tissues faster than others and also exit those tissues according to an equivalently shorter or longer time constant. He then designed a set of stepped decompression tables. For each step, the maximum distance a diver could ascend was set at the precise point where the breathing mix contained half the nitrogen pressure of the tissue that was, at that moment, the most saturated. This was called the leading tissue. After waiting for a set time, the diver could ascend to a new ceiling or decompression stop, and so on until the next stop was the surface.

Haldane's theory was not uniformly accepted and some scientists disagreed, including Leonard Hill and Frederick Keayes, the lead physician on the New York City tunnel works at the time. They thought a more linear approach or a different type of stepped procedure would work better. However, the British Admiralty accepted Haldane's proposal and his tables were subsequently adopted almost universally.

It is important to note that these tables were not developed using human subjects and that Haldane's human validation dives were only performed with a limited number of subjects and on a limited number of dive profiles. Other dive profiles were not tested, just extrapolated from adjacent profiles.

It was not long before Haldane and others started tweaking the dive tables in order to try and shorten the length of time divers needed to decompress. The allowable super-saturation ratio, originally defined by Haldane as 2:1, was reduced to 1.53:1 to account for nitrogen only. More tissues were added, with longer half-times. Haldane's original slowest tissue had a 75-minute half-time. Subsequently, there were tissues with half times of over 635 minutes. All these changes were field tested, mostly by young, fit Navy divers.

Although these dive tables proved to be generally effective, it was accepted that they would have a failure rate of approximately 1%, meaning that even if the tables were followed to the letter, sometimes decompression sickness would ensue.

The unpredictable nature of DCS had been recognised very early on and the official US Navy Diving Manual stipulated that dives requiring mandatory decompression stops were to be the exception, not the rule, and could only be carried out:

> *"when dictated by operational necessity and with the specific approval of the Commanding Officer or the Officer-in-Charge".* Also: *"scuba diving shall not be conducted to depths deeper than 100ft unless a recompression chamber is on station".*

We cannot know for sure what the true rate of incidence of DCS is, as it depends on what sort of diving is being done as well as many other factors. For recreational divers, the incidence has been estimated by DAN America and Europe to lie anywhere between 1 in 2500 and 1 in 35,000 dives, depending on the type of diving performed.

## Symptom Patterns

Experience and scientific reports show that some symptoms of decompression sickness arise more often after certain dive depth-time profiles than others. Articular pain symptoms in limbs, for instance, are more frequently observed after long dives to relatively shallow depths of 15 to 20m (50 to 66ft), often after exercise involving the limb in question. On the other hand, lower spinal cord symptoms, such as paralysis and bladder dysfunction, seem to arise more often after deeper (40m / 132ft) bounce dives. However, while these observations can be attributed to the saturation-desaturation behaviour of the affected tissues, they cannot be relied upon blindly.

Any symptom that presents itself within hours after surfacing from a dive with a certain degree of inert gas saturation should be considered decompression-related unless another, more obvious, cause can be pinpointed. In some DCS cases, symptoms have not appeared until 24 hours or more after a dive.

## Ignorance and denial

This no doubt explains why many divers, when confronted with possible DCS symptoms, find it hard to believe what is happening to them.

Most divers know that treating decompression sickness involves evacuation followed by a rather lengthy treatment in a recompression chamber. This makes some people more inclined to wait and hope that their symptoms will disappear rather than act. Factors that may influence this decision may also include the quality of the local healthcare system, whether or not they have health and travel insurance, the severity of the symptoms and the remoteness of the location.

Peer pressure can be involved in the non-reporting of DCS symptoms. This is understandable. Some divers think that their dive buddies will regard the fact that they have DCS as a sign of weakness or incompetence, even though all divers learn in their training that even if you adhere to the rules, there is no guarantee that you will not get DCS. In other instances, divers may be reluctant to request emergency evacuation so as not to spoil their friends' holiday.

Other divers may be unwilling to admit that they did not get enough sleep, drank alcohol the night before or used recreational drugs before a dive. An anonymous survey conducted some years ago by Dr Adel Taher and colleagues among tourist divers and dive instructors in Egypt revealed that alcohol and substance abuse in the community is very common, suggesting a relaxed attitude towards diving safety.

Having said this, there is no scientific evidence of a direct causal relationship between alcohol or substance abuse and decompression sickness.

Dive professionals may have financial reasons not to seek treatment, as someone who is diagnosed with DCS is usually advised not to dive for some time afterwards and no work means no pay. In 2000 Brubakk and Eftedal presented data from questionnaires returned by 740 recreational divers, 365 professional divers and 112 saturation divers in Norway.

They found that 19% of the recreational divers, 50% of professional divers and 63% of saturation divers had experienced symptoms of DCS that they never reported nor sought treatment for. In 2003, Hagberg and Ornhagen presented the results of an anonymous questionnaire circulated among dive masters and instructors in Sweden. These showed that the true incidence of DCS was almost 10 times higher than the official figure. This was due to a wait-and-see attitude or deliberate non-reporting.

The nature of DCS itself may be at fault. In the case of serious DCS, why would nitrogen bubbles be present only in certain lower spinal cord tissues? Maybe the bubbles also affect the brain? How else can you explain the fact that paralysed or nauseous, vomiting divers will often insist that everything is OK and choose to go to sleep rather than accept oxygen first aid?

Surely this is not the normal behaviour of an intelligent, trained adult.

Rather, it is reminiscent of so-called "frontal-lobe" behaviour, which occurs when the brain's frontal lobe has been damaged by trauma or bleeding. Apart from other personality changes, affected individuals may typically become insolent and reject obvious conclusions in favour of less likely but more easily acceptable alternatives.

The exact influence of diving and DCS on brain function has only been partially described and explored. Massive cerebral DCS obviously has an effect on the mind and therefore decision-making behaviour, resulting in somnolence, apathy, and central motor disturbance. But it is also entirely possible that the brain is affected to different degrees after diving.

Nitrogen accumulation may be responsible for the fatigue most divers feel after a couple of days of intensive diving. Recent research indicates that, contrary to what divers are taught, the effects of nitrogen narcosis do not disappear as soon as a diver leaves narcotic depths, but may persist for at least half an hour after the diver has surfaced. Read more about this in the next chapter.

### Factors Known to Increase DCS Susceptibility

Apart from nitrogen pressure and dive duration, there are other factors that influence why some divers bubble while others do not. Some of these factors have to do with how much nitrogen is absorbed during the dive and how fast and efficiently it is off-gassed during ascent. Inert gas is transported from the lungs to the tissues by the bloodstream so the speed and quantity of blood flowing to the tissues is important. Physical effort underwater increases the risk of DCS because the heart pumps more nitrogen-loaded blood into the tissues.

However, like on-gassing, the off-gassing process also depends on the rate of blood flow. So, at the end of the dive, when divers do their decompression stops, it is not a good idea for them to be completely at rest, hanging on the deco bar or suspended splendidly motionless at the stop depth. This is because, as the heart rate drops, there is a slowdown in the flow of blood and good blood flow is necessary to bring nitrogen out of the tissues and back to the lungs. For a safe decompression, off-gassing must be balanced with on-gassing. If you are mobile on your dive and immobile at your stop depth, there is no balance.

The relationship between cold and heat is relevant here too. The human body's response to cold is peripheral vasoconstriction. The diameter of the blood vessels closest to the skin decreases and blood flow is shifted to the core tissues to preserve body heat. This is why your skin becomes colder and paler. Subcutaneous tissues are also affected. Usually, at the beginning of a dive in cold or cool water, your thermal protection is adequate, your vasoconstriction reflex does not come into play and your tissues become loaded with nitrogen in the normal way.

Near the end of the dive, however, as cold sets in, you begin vasoconstricting. As you ascend to your decompression stop, the cold causes changes in tissue perfusion that slow off-gassing. US Navy experiments have shown that performing a dive in warm water and then decompressing in cooler water carries at least five times more risk of DCS than diving in cold water and decompressing in warmer water.

Many divers are colder when they are doing their decompression stops than when they are diving at depth. Then they further increase their risk of DCS by staying immobile while they do their deco and doing as little deco as possible so that they can surface as quickly as possible and warm up. This is not wise.

### "Ideal" vs. "Improvised" DCS management: Diving in remote or holiday locations vs. diving at home

If you look at people's diving habits when they are at home compared to when they are on vacation, you will notice striking differences. In some cases, you would think you were looking at completely different people.

When you dive at home, you usually spend plenty of time preparing for the dive. You know the dive site well because you dive it often. You also probably have tools and spare equipment with you in case something breaks. When you go on holiday, baggage weight and size limitations prevent you from carrying spare equipment, although you know that the equipment offered by operators in remote areas may not be very good.

On vacation, you may not be as disciplined concerning your health as you are at home. You may drink more than usual or take drugs the evening before a dive or even on the dive day itself. Needless to say, diving while under the influence increases the risk of an accident and not just because of physiological issues. Behaviour change can be a factor too.

You may have had little sleep. You may be suffering from jet lag and dehydration because of the flight, air conditioning, diarrhoea, and or alcohol use. You may be seasick and less able to control your buoyancy on your safety stop.

Diving holidays are not cheap. After spending a long time just getting to your dream destination, you are understandably anxious not to miss out on anything. Every dive booked MUST be dived. At home, it is easy to skip a dive if you do not feel well. On holiday, it is much more difficult.

Finally, at home, you will rarely do so many dives in such a short space of time. Multi-day repetitive diving for a week or more, without a day off, is often a factor in so-called "unearned" or "unexplained" DCS incidents. Dive computers may have impressive specifications but there is no way they can accurately predict your off-gassing rate, certainly not after you have surfaced. Computers do not know your heart condition or breathing rate. They cannot tell if you are young or old, fit or unfit, fat or thin. They have no idea what physical activity you do between dives, nor do they know how well or poorly hydrated you are.

Even the very latest dive computer models are capable of calculating a decompression schedule for only two repetitive dives at most. Anything beyond that, even if it can be calculated, depends on so many unknown factors that you should follow the computer's recommendations only with extreme caution. In fact, depending on the risk you are willing to take, it may be wiser not to do a third dive, or dive really conservatively and only after a long surface interval. It is also good advice to take a day off every three diving days to reset yourself. After this prolonged off-gassing period, you can start afresh.

What about all these dive guides and instructors who seemingly do nothing but dive, dive, dive? How do they manage? There are two possible explanations for this. Perhaps, somehow, they are more resistant to decompression bubble formation. After all, we know that individual differences exist and some divers do produce more bubbles than others. Some older divers seem not to suffer any ill effects from a lifelong career of intensive diving.

However, they may be a self-selected community, with their less-DCS-resistant contemporaries having given up the sport earlier in life. Alternatively, it may be that the fact of diving day in, day out, year in, year out, by some unknown yet-to-be-discovered mechanism, protects a diver from DCS. Because neither of these hypotheses is as yet proven, it has to be assumed that, statistically, all divers are at risk at some point of getting DCS.

## How best to manage DCS

DCS cannot be predicted precisely and, even if the risk seems very small for certain dive profiles, the chance of getting DCS is never zero, so it is best to prepare for the eventuality. This means that you need an emergency plan.

Diving accident first aid is taught by DAN and many other agencies and organisations. It is not complicated. The priority always is to check and control the ABCs, airway, breathing and circulation. Then, administer oxygen and fluids. Finally, evacuate the patient to a hyperbaric facility.

The actual recompression treatment administered to a diver with DCS may vary considerably depending on local circumstances, technical limitations and the experience of medical staff. It is very difficult to compare the outcomes of different treatment tables, as DCS is relatively rare and each case is different. Therefore, there is no point in discussing what constitutes the best hyperbaric treatment.

All you can say for sure is that recompression treatment with oxygen is better than no recompression treatment at all or recompression treatment using air only. And any recompression treatment should be carried out in a safe way that does not involve further risk to the patient.

If you know what you need to provide first aid in cases of suspected DCS, you can make the necessary preparations. You need basic life support equipment as well as sufficient oxygen and fluids. You also need to have a means of emergency communication and know how to get an injured diver to the nearest hyperbaric chamber as quickly as possible.

Really, all this should be part of the preparation for any dive. Nevertheless, many divers choose to dive in places and with operations that have none of these preparations in place. Statistically, on most dives there are no problems, but, once in a while, something will go wrong and someone will suffer.

## DCS Management in remote areas

In remote areas, many of the easy things about scuba diving become more difficult. Arranging to have emergency supplies of oxygen, fluids and medication on hand is a little more complicated. You can't prepare your own contingency plans for a diving holiday in a remote area. All you can do is rely on local structures already in place.

Of course, some places are more remote than others. An example of an effective local structure can be found in the Red Sea Sinai region in Egypt, where there is a Hyperbaric Medical Centre that was built by the Egyptian Ministry of Tourism in March 1993. This was the first independent hyperbaric centre established specifically for recreational divers. As the diving industry in Egypt boomed, more and more private and hospital-based hyperbaric chambers were set up. In 2012, the South Sinai received almost one million recreational tourist divers. Today, there are 13 chambers across Sinai and the Egyptian Red Sea coast.

The Hyperbaric Medical Centre began life as a multi-place, multi-lock recompression chamber in a strategically chosen location a short distance from the harbour and search and rescue facility. In 2011, it was upgraded with a modern 12-man chamber, fitted out with full vital sign monitoring equipment, a mechanical ventilator and a gas blending station to enable provision of the right gases for any treatment table.

The facility has fixed daily opening hours but also operates a 24-hour emergency local and international hotline that is always manned. Physicians live on the premises and one is always on duty. The Centre serves as the headquarters for DAN Egypt and has an excellent reputation in the area. It also serves the local community, providing treatment for non-diving-related medical problems, and advises governmental law-making bodies and the Ministry of Tourism.

In 2012, the Hyperbaric Medical Centre dealt with around 80 diving accidents where divers required recompression and over 400 where recompression was not necessary. It also handled around 1800 other diving injuries and requests for medical attention. Problems ranged from ear barotrauma, marine animal injuries and mild cases requiring only oxygen at surface pressure, to surgical repair and management of minor trauma.

The Centre also provides diving fitness assessments and counselling. It has several backup generators and its own ambulance. It works with local search and rescue teams, cooperates with governmental and private hospitals and shares medical data with other institutions worldwide. The resident physician also deals with emergency diving medical inquiries from the Southern Red Sea and the Middle East via the hotline. Two permanent diving medical specialists and a dedicated hyperbaric technician are on staff. Medical personnel from around the world visit the centre for training and take part in research. Since the arrival of the second chamber, the centre can now provide hyperbaric oxygen treatment for non-diving related conditions as well as for experimental research. The transfer of patients to higher tertiary hospitals in Cairo or the patient's home country is possible by land or air ambulance.

All staff members receive paramedic training and the centre regularly undergoes auditing under the Recompression Chamber Assistance & Partnership Program, a joint initiative of all five International DAN organisations. Financially, the centre is dependent on the generation of revenue from diving cases. Statistically around 20% of patients are not covered by insurance and are treated for free.

The centre works with the Chamber of Diving and Water Sports and the Ministry of Tourism to set rules and regulations regarding safety standards for dive operations. The requirements include oxygen and radio communications on board dive boats.

Certain other regions, such as the Maldives and the Azores, have similarly efficient systems. In other areas, there may just be a recompression chamber in a local medical facility. In some places, medical centres already have a heavy local workload and resources, gases and supplies can be limited and/or very expensive. Furthermore, transport problems may obstruct rapid transfer to a treatment facility.

The success of a remote, non-hospital-based hyperbaric centre depends on the local professional diving community. Dive operators should know whether or not the centre has an intensive care unit or cardiac critical care ward (this is unlikely) and be conscious of the fact that evacuation without proper first aid compromises the ultimate effect of any treatment. Awareness and prevention of DCS are the key strategies and dive centres should pass on to their guests information as to exactly what services are available locally. Unfortunately, they do not always do this.

Obtaining a proper and detailed medical history, evaluating the patients' diving profiles as far back as possible and analysing the patient's lifestyle are key factors in arriving at a diagnosis. There are two aspects to a patient's lifestyle. The first deals with their vocational activities and the type of job they have, and the second deals with their lifestyle while on vacation. Some people may not usually smoke a lot or drink much alcohol at home, but on vacation, they tend to smoke and drink more.

It is best if diving medical specialists are divers themselves. This helps them gain the trust of their patients, gives them greater credibility and creates a special relationship between patient and physician. Knowledge of local dive sites and an understanding of the environmental conditions also help the physician verify the patient's story and analyse the dive accident.

Triage principles in remote areas differ a little from the conventional textbooks. The priority is the patient's well-being. The same questions arise all the time. Will the patient be better off if they are transferred? Can transport be arranged efficiently and safely? If the patient is transported by air, is the cabin pressurized and how many take-offs and landings will be involved? In many regions, the geo-political situation may influence the answers to these questions.

When discussing the triage of diving accidents, it is important to take into account the availability and proximity of higher-level medical facilities. If possible, patients that require intensive care, life support equipment, such as mechanical ventilators, or advanced diagnostic machinery, should be stabilized and moved immediately on oxygen to the nearest hospital. They should remain there until they are stable enough to be treated in the hyperbaric chamber and then transported home.

Once a patient is received, any life-threatening condition is dealt with first. Then they receive an initial hyperbaric medical treatment. Depending on their clinical condition, their response, the limitations of the recompression chamber, the availability of other therapy required and other factors, a decision is taken on whether to move them to a specialized centre. In some areas, the physician has to consider the effects of a prolonged sea journey before reaching an airport. Helicopter medevac is not always available and long drives over mountainous passes can involve significant variation in altitude.

These are all factors to be considered when deciding to move a patient from one place to another. Field experience suggests that 90% of patients can be medevac'd by air in a pressurized cabin following their third bout of recompression. Patients are usually advised to wait 72 hours after their last hyperbaric treatment before they fly.

## The International Divers Alert Network Recompression Chamber Assistance & Partnership Programme (IDANRCAPP)

In remote areas, there may be no recompression services at all, or existing facilities may not be particularly sophisticated and grossly underfunded due to limited utilisation. The International Divers Alert Network (IDAN) Recompression Chamber Assistance & Partnership Program (RCAPP) was developed as an outreach initiative to assist under-funded and/or under-supported hyperbaric treatment facilities, usually located in remote areas and dedicated to the treatment of recreational diving injuries and emergencies.

The goals of the RCAPP are to ensure that remote chambers comply as far as possible with the IDAN Risk Assessment Guide and help them reach a minimum level of technical and operational quality. Contact with and visits by RCAPP staff also help to update and expand the DAN hyperbaric oxygen chamber database so that divers know what is available. They also make local dive operators aware of the need for good hyperbaric chamber facilities. By collaborating with local hospitals and local dive operators, safety is improved and the cost of remote emergency hyperbaric treatment is reduced.

The core of the RCAPP is the internationally accepted and widely used IDAN Risk Assessment Guide for Recompression Facilities, first published in 1999 and now available in English, Spanish and Portuguese.

Facilities either apply for RCAPP assistance, or the regional DAN office identifies suitable and deserving chambers. Once a facility enters the program, an initial site assessment is performed, which is focused on determining the facility's essential needs. DAN engineering and operations professionals perform a risk-based assessment of equipment, operations, staffing, procedures and documentation. A detailed and comprehensive report is then compiled and given to the facility to help staff achieve compliance with minimum international safety requirements. Based on the assessment of needs, additional support may extend to providing essential equipment, guiding facility upgrades, offering a range of physician and staff training programmes and helping to meet essential maintenance requirements.

There has been significant improvement in skills as a result of DAN-sponsored or coordinated training efforts. The RCAPP now includes 112 facilities in 54 countries, spread across the diving world. The vast majority of chambers are multiplace, meaning that staff members can provide hands-on assistance inside the chamber during treatments.

Most facilities can even offer advanced treatments using deeper tables or using mixed gases to provide safer excursions at depth. Only around 15% have had significant problems that could lead to compromised levels of care, and these problems have been addressed through guidance, technical consultation and financial assistance.

DAN has provided training in the form of chamber attendant & operator courses and acrylic window and general maintenance courses. Training support has also been given to about half of the facilities. About 20% of facilities have received equipment grants.

The RCAPP is funded in the main through the various DAN mission departments, but donations, individual patrons and fundraising are also part of the overall strategy.

DAN has analysed the information gathered from its extensive assessment and outreach efforts and has concluded that, by extending this initiative more fully into all DAN regions, it would be able to expand support and make the best use of the experience and expertise available within the various regions.

An IDAN Chamber Certification Programme, based on a common approach to compliance, is planned for the near future.

## Telephone assistance

Divers, their buddies and their family members experience a great deal of stress when faced with the possibility of DCS. They don't know what will happen, they worry over incorrect or insufficient treatment and fear the consequences. Will the diver be paralysed? Will they have bladder problems? Will they have difficulty walking? Will they go deaf? Will they die?

Sometimes, the local dive centre can help. Unfortunately, however, some dive centre personnel are either unwilling to get involved or try to explain away symptoms as not being decompression-related. This may be because they fear that they might be held responsible for running an "unsafe" dive. Nevertheless, the injured diver will still be apprehensive and frightened. Fortunately, getting help via a telephone call is now possible wherever you are in the world. Even if you are in an area not covered by a mobile network, you can always use a satellite phone.

DAN has used call-centre technology since the early days. On five continents, regional DAN offices (America, Europe, Southern Africa, Asia-Pacific and Japan) provide a 24/7, 365 days per year service not only to those who have a DAN membership but to any diver in need. The diver's story is quickly assessed and a tentative working diagnosis is established. Then, first aid directions and counselling as to the best way to get adequate care are given.

Needless to say, this is easier when the diver is in, say, southern France than if they are floating on a liveaboard in the Andaman Sea south of India, three days away from the nearest port.

The definition of "best way" depends on what means are available at that moment and in that place. Sometimes there is a need to improvise. The hotline doctors need to be experienced enough to be able to look ahead. They may take decisions that divert from what should be the best way, simply because that way is not possible.

Often they have to select the next best option. However, even if optimal help is not available, it is of great benefit for the injured diver to be able to talk over the phone in their own language to someone who understands what is happening, knows what the diver is going through, and can provide advice, comfort and understanding.

## In-water recompression treatment

An option considered by some divers who frequently dive in remote areas is recompression treatment in the water. After all, the three principles of DCS treatment are pressure, oxygen, and as soon as possible. This is what in-water recompression treatment provides: pressure, oxygen (if available) and action taken very soon after the appearance of symptoms. Two out of three, and sometimes three of three, can't be bad, can it?

The most widely described in-water recompression procedure is the one that has been developed and published by Carl Edmonds and his team in Australia. It has been standardised and conditions for its use have been established. Briefly, it involves sending the injured diver down to 9m (30ft), preferably with a full-face mask and a supply of oxygen from the surface via a long hose. The diver remains at this depth for 30 minutes, then, depending on the evolution of the symptoms, either stays a further half hour or more or begins to ascend, taking 120 minutes to reach the surface.

This means the diver is submerged at potentially toxic oxygen depths for at least 60 minutes. The pressure at 9m (30ft) is 1.9 ATA, and breathing pure oxygen at this pressure can cause convulsions. In some cases, a diver with progressing neurological symptoms may be left alone underwater in a situation where it is difficult to evaluate them, and difficult to assist them.

A prolonged underwater stay almost immediately after surfacing from a dive can result in other physiological problems. Dehydration is one of them. Scuba divers are almost always dehydrated at the end of a dive. Technical divers who hydrate themselves underwater are the exception.

In severe cases of DCS, sometimes up to 6 litres of intravenous fluids are needed to combat shock. This is difficult to achieve while the injured diver is underwater. Body temperature is another factor. Usually, the thermal protection of a wetsuit is only just enough to maintain body temperature for the duration of a dive. Putting a diver back in the water for a further 1.5 to 3.5 hours without a dry suit can result in hypothermia even in tropical waters.

Most of these problems can be avoided if in-water recompression is properly planned, prepared, practised and executed. In certain situations, a diving emergency plan may involve in-water recompression.

If so, all the necessary equipment must be on site, deployed and tested in realistic situations. All divers and staff must have been trained in its deployment and use and the system must be set up before the dive or be able to be set up within minutes when needed. This is why, practically speaking, the use of in-water compression as an emergency option is limited to scientific diving, military operations, or well-organised expeditions.

If these conditions are all met, then, in remote areas, in-water recompression may be the best option.

If the conditions are not met then sending an injured diver back into the water may do more harm than good.

The number of cases where in-water recompression is beneficial may be very limited. In mild cases of DCS, the benefit of in-water recompression is probably minor. In very severe cases the potential harm and risks are probably too great to attempt it.

Even though recreational divers tell stories of instances of successful in-water recompression; even though some dive training agencies even teach courses in it; and even though you can get plenty of "how-to" advice on the Internet, nevertheless diving medicine specialists are seriously dubious about the value of in-water recompression, except when the stringent conditions outlined above are in place.

### Evacuation strategies

A 2004 workshop on the management of mild (or marginal) DCS in remote areas came up with recommendations as to when emergency evacuation should be carried out at all costs and when it may be better not to evacuate a patient but instead use the best non-hyperbaric treatment available.

Using a very precise definition of mild DCS, the panel agreed that if the patient's condition does not worsen after 24 hours then the risk of further deterioration is virtually non-existent. This means that in cases with no neurological impairment or symptoms such as shock (as verified in person by a competent paramedical or medical professional), the effort, risk and expense of organising a fully pressurised air evacuation or a prolonged land or sea evacuation are probably not justified.

This suggests that prompt evacuation is not always the only or even the best option and this is a concept that stirs controversy even among diving doctors.

In many cases, it is unrealistic to expect that there will always be a way to get someone to the hyperbaric chamber within hours of a DCS hit. Sometimes it just can't be done.

Neither can you assume that there are unlimited funds available. A story comes to mind of a diver on a cruise in the deep south of the Red Sea who was suffering from severe joint pain caused by DCS. The boat was three days' sail away from the nearest port. The injured diver expected that a helicopter would come and pick him up immediately in the middle of the night.

That just isn't possible.

Decisions as to whether to evacuate a patient and where to evacuate the patient to need to be taken in light of the symptoms, their possible evolution, the time needed to organise an evacuation, and the costs involved. Only then can you judge if it is really an option worth pursuing.

### Delay in recompression treatment

Despite modern communications technology and diver education, the delay in recompressing bent divers can still be surprisingly long, even in places like Europe, where transportation options are good. Some of the diver-related reasons for this were discussed earlier in this chapter.

Other reasons are more medically oriented. Often, divers are first examined by medical personnel who are not trained or experienced in diving medicine. Also, when DCS symptoms appear outside normal working hours, emergency response medical personnel may not have the immediate backup of other, more experienced doctors. In our modern technological society, this often results in laboratory tests and scans being prescribed followed by a long wait for results.

Statistics compiled by DAN and other teams show that fewer than 50% of patients with DCS are recompressed within 6 hours of symptoms appearing. This does not seem to have changed substantially in the last 15 years.

## DCS outcome

Even if the delay before recompression treatment could be made shorter, by how much should it be reduced? Jordi Desola and his team conducted an interesting study. They found that in Southern Europe there was no difference in outcome if a diver was recompressed within 6 hours or later.

This seemed difficult to accept but the general conclusions were later confirmed by further similar surveys in the UK and France.

It seems that a "golden hour" for obtaining the best results does not actually exist, probably because DCS, once present, rapidly triggers biochemical and biophysical reactions and becomes a systemic disease rather than just a bubble disease. Of course, this should not be taken as proof that rapid evacuation for early recompression treatment should not be recommended.

The words to live by are still:

*"the sooner the better, but not at the cost of quality".*

It does however argue against spending enormous amounts of money to evacuate a diver if DCS has already been present for several hours and if the evacuation is going to take more than a day anyway.

Generally speaking, about 30 % of all DCS-stricken divers suffer some sort of residual outcome even after full and timely hyperbaric treatment. Optimal first aid with intravenous fluid administration and oxygen seems to improve the final results, although this is very difficult to prove scientifically as it would require a high number of comparable cases with good documentation of treatment and outcome.

Some forms of DCS produce more long-term effects than others. A German report found that almost all patients who suffered inner ear DCS had permanent damage, despite receiving optimal treatment.

Type I DCS produces bone and joint lesions and these seem to be becoming more common, due to the growth of technical diving. These effects may not be detected for several years after the initial lesion.

Neurological DCS often does not heal completely. However, following a good and comprehensive rehabilitation programme, involving the recruitment of nerve pathways, for at least two years may result in a return to almost normal function. While this may be good news, it is naive to think that functional recovery equates to a cure. It is simply a case of the body using some of its existing spare parts.

## Returning to diving after DCS

Although, after a brush with DCS, many divers swear that they are never going to dive again, experience suggests that, six months or so later, they will be asking when they can get back in the water again.

There are a number of possible answers to this question and it depends on the diver. The easiest thing to do is just to follow the rule book and tell them that, if they have permanent damage, they should never dive again.

However, telling experienced divers with post-DCS injury not to dive contrasts sharply with our willingness to allow young children, very old people or people with motor or mental disabilities to scuba dive, albeit with certain limitations and precautions. Would an experienced diver with a similar handicap not be safer in the water than a novice?

There are two key questions.

- 1. Is the handicap such that diving is still possible anatomically and physiologically, without compromising the diver's safety?
- 2. Is the diver aware of the risk and consequences of having another diving accident?

The first question is more of a medical decision. The second question can only be answered following a psychological appraisal of the diver. An assessment of the diver's personality, risk awareness and ability to accept limitations cannot be achieved by one single examination. It requires repeated contact throughout the treatment and rehabilitation process.

The advice given should be tailored to the individual and the decision should only be made some time after treatment has been completed, to allow time to observe how the diver handles their new circumstances.

A key consideration is if the diver can still obtain diving insurance despite their history of DCS.

In the end, the diver will make their own decision, and you can only hope that it is taken in full knowledge and understanding of the consequences, risks and limitations.

**Take-home messages**

- Judging from what we know now, DCS will never be entirely preventable.
- DCS first aid and treatment in remote areas may be extremely challenging.
- DCS First Aid is important to achieve better results.

- Reaching a diagnosis of DCS is sometimes difficult in remote areas, and requires a good analysis of all data collected.
- Even in optimal circumstances, DCS treatment does not guarantee a full recovery without lasting effects.

11

# NITROGEN NARCOSIS

By: Pierre Lafère, Cecile Lavoute, Walter Hemelryck

WHEN DIVERS TALK ABOUT NITROGEN NARCOSIS, THEY sometimes refer to a concept known as "Martini's Law," which states that for every 9m to 15m (30ft to 50ft) of depth, a diver experiences the narcotic effect of drinking one martini on an empty stomach. The comparison of nitrogen narcosis with a feeling of pleasant drunkenness is generally recognized as being an apt one. As with alcohol, the effects of narcosis can differ from one diver to another depending on their fitness and mental state.

However, nitrogen narcosis is a serious concern. To operate effectively underwater, a diver has to master a considerable number of different skills that rely on manual dexterity, motor coordination and both short-term and long-term memory. These skills are essential to staying safe in situations where precise actions and accurate judgement are required.

Divers are more likely to experience narcosis than decompression sickness. Indeed, according to a survey by psychiatrist David F. Colvard, 20% of male and 18 % of female divers admit to suffering from signs or symptoms of nitrogen narcosis. These symptoms include dizziness, euphoria, excitement, poor coordination, slowness of thought, bad judgement or careless attitude. Yet the underlying mechanisms of nitrogen narcosis are less well understood even than those of decompression sickness.

## The Physics

Recreational scuba divers normally use compressed air, which contains 78.09% nitrogen, 20.95% oxygen, 0.039% carbon dioxide, and small traces of other rare gases (argon, neon, hydrogen, xenon, krypton, and ozone) or pollutant gases. Air also contains a variable amount of water vapour, around 1%. When breathed, oxygen diffuses through the lungs into the bloodstream and is carried to all tissues where it is metabolised and used for the production of energy.

Nitrogen and the other gases follow the same route, but, unlike oxygen, nitrogen is not metabolised, which is why it is commonly referred to as an inert gas. It accumulates within the body until, in accordance with Henry's Law, there is a state of equilibrium between the nitrogen pressure in inspired air and the nitrogen pressure inside each tissue.

Dalton's Law states that, with increasing depth and pressure, the partial pressure of each component gas in the air we breathe will increase proportionally, resulting in increased diffusion from the bloodstream into the tissues. Since an inert gas is not altered or metabolised by the body, the effects of nitrogen in our cells are directly proportional to its partial pressure. There comes a point where the partial pressure reaches a threshold, beyond which symptoms become apparent. After that, symptoms increase as the partial pressure increases.

Everyone is affected by narcosis to some extent when they dive deep. Responsiveness can differ from person to person, but it is commonly accepted that the effects begin around 30m (100ft), although some people may experience effects of narcosis from 21m (70ft). As the pressure increases, signs and symptoms become more severe and can eventually lead to loss of consciousness.

Different gases have different narcotic power. Traditionally, nitrogen is given a relative narcotic power of 1 and is used as the reference by which other gases are compared. Several authors have developed scales of narcotic potency but Brauer ´s scale is the one most commonly used. Many attempts have been made to correlate the narcotic potency of gases to their physical properties and it seems that the best correlation has been obtained with lipid solubility; the more soluble a gas is, the more easily it can migrate and dissolve into nerve cells.

## Understanding nitrogen narcosis

### History

The first description of what was possibly nitrogen narcosis came in 1822 when French physicist Louis-Théodore Colladon told the story of his descent in a diving bell, saying that he "*was in a state of excitement resembling the effect of some spirituous liquor*". However, it was not until 1859 that J.B. Green, an American professional diver, gave an accurate description of the signs and symptoms of narcosis during dives to 45m (150ft) and beyond. Green's account referred to a sense of excitement followed by numbness, hallucinations and impaired judgment.

Paul Bert, well known for his work on oxygen toxicity and decompression sickness, also briefly mentioned the narcotic potential of air breathed under pressure, as did his contemporaries C.C.G. Damant, A.E. Boycott and Haldane.

In the early 1930s, having found during experimental dives to depths of 60m to 106m (200ft to 350ft), that in 17 out 58 dives the diver experienced "*partial loss of consciousness*", the British Royal Navy conducted a thorough investigation. The problem was regarded as serious because they did not know what was causing it.

Although the divers continued to give all the correct hand signals, after decompression, they could not recall what had happened during the dive.

It was not until 1935 that Behnke and his colleagues correctly associated these signs and symptoms with the raised partial pressure of nitrogen and the concept of nitrogen narcosis was born. Jacques Cousteau dubbed it "l'ivresse des profondeurs" or "the drunkenness of the depths".

### Signs and symptoms

Nitrogen narcosis impairs nervous system functions that may affect a diver's ability to act effectively or even survive the dive. To recognise all the performance impairments and to understand the underlying mechanisms, it is useful to categorise and classify the different signs and symptoms.

Originally, Behnke and his colleagues divided the effects of narcosis into three main categories, that come into play as nitrogen pressure increases:

- 1) emotional reactions,
- 2) impairment of higher mental processes, and
- 3) impairment of neuromuscular control.

### Contributing factors

As the underwater environment in which divers operate is markedly different from the surface environment, it seems logical that environmental factors should influence performance. The diving community has cited several factors as contributing to the onset and severity of narcosis, albeit often without much scientific evidence.

For example, increased partial pressures of $CO_2$ from hard work or heavy swimming are believed to enlarge cerebral vessels leading to a higher nitrogen presence in the brain. Other supposed risk factors include alcohol use, being hungover, fatigue, anxiety or apprehension, the effects of motion sickness medication, rate of descent, task loading and time pressure stress.

From a scientific point of view, the available evidence for most of these factors is not particularly strong. This is because experiments have not been appropriately designed to allow a clear determination of the direction and size of the effects. Moreover, claims about whether something exacerbates or reduces narcosis are often based on fuzzy criteria. Current evidence shows that only ethanol and amphetamines, respectively, increase or alleviate the signs and symptoms of narcosis.

These issues are not just of academic concern. Lack of clarity in this field has probability contributed to divers being given some dubious advice. Avoiding the contributory factors that you can control, such as fatigue and alcohol, and minimising the impact of those factors you cannot control, by choosing appropriate equipment or being prepared to cancel a dive when it doesn't seem safe, may not be enough to prevent narcosis. These steps will obviously help reduce the effects but, even so, narcosis can still strike a diver at depths where it has not struck them before.

### Recent insights (1970s to present)

Two theories have attempted to explain the symptoms associated with narcosis. These are the "lipid" and the "proteinic" theories.

### Lipid theory

In the early 20$^{th}$ century, Meyer and Overton observed that the narcotic potency of inert gases and volatile anaesthetics was linked to their affinity with lipids and their capacity to dissolve through the lipid membrane of cells. By saturating the lipid bilayer of cell membranes, the narcotic gas was believed to increase the membrane's thickness. Although the Meyer-Overton hypothesis did not account for transport processes, which were not known about at the time, it worked well for molecules that just crossed the lipid membrane by simple diffusion

According to the hypothesis, the expansion of the lipid membrane in the brain disrupted nerve impulses. Symptoms of narcosis would then occur as the passage of information was interrupted.

However, in 1978, it was established that an anaesthetic concentration of narcotic gases did not in fact modify the volume or thickness of the cell membrane. Other experiments carried out by COMEX and the French Navy to study high-pressure nervous syndrome (HPNS), using helium-nitrogen-oxygen (trimix) and helium-hydrogen-oxygen (hydreliox) mixtures, showed that the lipid theory does not explain disorders caused by gases under pressure and that another mechanism must therefore be involved.

### Proteinic theory

More recently, Nicholas Franks and William Lieb of Imperial College, London, suggested that gases with high narcotic power (such as xenon) bind to the membrane proteins of cells.

Further work on behavioural changes at different speeds of compression supports this idea. The main targets are cerebral receptors and ionic channels, both of which are involved in neuronal cell communication.

When gas molecules bind to these membrane proteins, they act like a drug. The use of pharmacological molecules preventing the binding of the gas to these receivers should therefore be able to negate their effect and help identify the underlying mechanisms of narcosis.

Since the early 2000s, studies of neurotransmission in the brain structures involved in the control of motor and cognitive processes (the basal ganglia) have shown both nitrogen and pressure combining in this binding process.

Pressure activates inhibitory receptors in several brain areas and this releases an abundance of dopamine, an excitatory neurotransmitter, in the striatum, increasing motor activity and the activity of the thalamocortical pathway. This could be the cause of some symptoms of HPNS.

Nitrogen, however, directly inhibits some excitatory neurons and, as a result, motor activity is slowed down. This could explain some of the symptoms of nitrogen narcosis.

## Measuring nitrogen narcosis objectively

The study of nitrogen narcosis has always been interdisciplinary, and physiological concepts have always influenced behavioural analysis. Experiments have therefore focused on behavioural development, such as the loss of the righting reflex in cats, or electrophysiological indices. Many studies are also performed in vitro, where change is measured at the cellular and/or biochemical level. With humans, efforts to quantify the effects of nitrogen narcosis can be roughly divided into two approaches.

The first is a behavioural approach, measuring task performance such as mental arithmetic, memory, reaction time and manual dexterity. Although these behavioural studies have confirmed progressive deterioration with increasing pressure, many of the tests have been criticised because motivation, experience and learning can influence the results.

The second approach relies on observing changes in objective, measurable neurological parameters. Ideally, these tests should be

- a) reproducible;
- b) less subject-and-investigator-dependent than a behavioural approach;
- c) based on observing changes in neurological parameters such as electro-encephalographic (EEG) recordings and the like, and
- d) easy to implement underwater.

## Critical Flicker Fusion Frequency (CFFF) studies

CFFF is a reliable, albeit indirect, indicator of brain function and under standard conditions it can be used to study cortical arousal in humans. It is defined as "the frequency at which a stimulus of intermittent light seems to be completely stable to the observer".

A single blue LED light enclosed in a smaller cylindrical container (to shield it from stray light and reflections) is presented to the test subject in a straight line at a distance of 50cm (20 inches).

The investigator turns a dial slowly to increase or decrease the flickering frequency. When the test subject indicates that no more flickering is perceived, that value is noted by the investigator. As there are no markings on the dial, nor any detectable starting point, the test subject cannot know the actual flicker frequency. This test is repeated three times and the average value is noted as the CFFF.

It has recently been shown that CFFF provides an assessment of cognitive function that is similar to some tests in the Psychology Experiment Building Language (PEBL) series. In tests specifically chosen to track deterioration in certain neurocognitive skills important to diving, such as visual-motor integration and co-ordination and visual memory, CFFF yielded remarkably consistent results both in a normobaric oxygen environment and in hyperbaric conditions at a depth of 30m (100ft) using air or nitrox 40.

Historical reports have suggested that there is a correlation between EEG and CFFF variations and changes in a diver's mental state. Also, changes in CFFF during a helium-oxygen dive to 630m (2070ft) showed systematic variations and a relationship between compression and pressure. These variations ran parallel to EEG modifications.

The CFFF is less complicated to set up than behavioural computer-based testing. A waterproof housing has recently been constructed, allowing the measurement of CFFF underwater. One dive computer manufacturer has implemented not only CFFF but also a limited set of neuropsychometric tests in one of their diving computer models for underwater scientific experiments. This might contribute to a better understanding of nitrogen narcosis.

Several recent studies have been conducted using CFFF. These were the first to measure the effects of nitrogen narcosis during an entire dive AND for some time after the diver surfaces.

One of the most remarkable observations was that, even if subjective feelings of narcosis may abate rapidly after surfacing, the actual cerebral impairment persists for at least 30 minutes.

This may be important in situations where precise and accurate judgment or actions are essential. Diver-training programs currently advise (based on lipid theory, which is now thought to be inaccurate) that in the event of nitrogen narcosis, divers should ascend a little for the narcotic effects to dissipate.

The CFFF studies show that this may not be either true or sufficient.

These studies also provide significant evidence that, objectively, nitrogen narcosis may be influenced just by pressure and the gas being breathed, rather than other contributory factors. In other words, it seems that, except perhaps in extreme cases, environmental factors have no major influence on the severity of cerebral impairment related to nitrogen narcosis.

Deep diving is associated with progressive deterioration of brain performance due to nitrogen narcosis. However, both

CFFF and behavioural computer-based testing have shown that this impairment is actually preceded by a performance improvement when divers arrive at depth.

In one experiment, divers were assessed by continuous recording of near-infrared spectroscopy (NIRS), a promising technology that measures hemodynamic signals from the brain. The values measured seemed to indicate that significant activation recorded in the prefrontal cortex was oxygen-dependent.

### Preventing nitrogen narcosis

Of the gases tested for Brauer's scale of narcotic potency, four are more narcotic than nitrogen. These are xenon, nitrous oxide, krypton and argon. Three, hydrogen, neon, and helium, are less narcotic than nitrogen and have been extensively studied for use in deep diving.

The use of helium-oxygen mixtures has enabled dives to be made to depths of 610m (2000ft) in a hyperbaric chamber and 460m (1500ft) in the open sea.

However, below 100m (330ft) divers have experienced behavioural problems such as trembling, cognitive impairment, and decreased psychomotor performances. These effects have been attributed to HPNS.

Neon was useless because it is so dense that divers had difficulty breathing it. Hydrogen presented numerous advantages. Its low molecular weight and low narcotic power limited HPNS and narcosis and made it easy to breathe.

Indeed, in a French experiment, a hydreliox (hydrogen, helium, and oxygen) cocktail allowed divers to reach a depth of 701m (2300ft). However, considerations of cost and logistical complexity make dives like this only possible for large offshore diving companies.

One interesting finding relates to the comparison of air and nitrox diving. When divers do not know beforehand, they cannot tell which gas they are breathing based just on the way they feel. However, computer-based behavioural assessments and CFFF show significant impairment of brain performance when breathing both.

No symptoms does not mean no nitrogen narcosis. (If you don't feel you're narked, it doesn't mean you aren't.)

This is an important thing for divers to know, as overestimation or underestimation of the severity of narcosis can be a real safety issue.

From a narcosis point of view, it could be better to choose nitrox as your breathing gas simply because success or failure can be determined by subjective considerations as well as objective factors.

It does seem that nitrox at least partially protects against decreased neuro-cognitive performance.

## Adaptation to nitrogen narcosis

Based on studies reporting significant improvement after initial performance deterioration, the diving community generally believes that divers can adapt to the signs and symptoms of nitrogen narcosis. Most experienced deep divers agree that they perform better when they carry out repeated and progressively deeper excursions on a cumulative basis.

Indeed, nitrogen narcosis can be controlled to a varying degree, but the way it affects an individual can change from day to day.

Studies carried out with saturation divers suggested that they might have developed some tolerance at storage depths of around 40m (130ft). However, divers that perform the same tasks over and over again gradually find them easier to do and this may lead them to think that they have developed narcosis tolerance.

A good analogy is habitual drunks who learn to cope with their impaired reflexes, cognitive functions and motor skills. The problem is, of course, that even though they may be able to perform tasks more effectively, they are still just as drunk.

Contrary to popular belief, sport divers do not develop tolerance to nitrogen narcosis. Although scientific results do produce conflicting results, they are generally unable to confirm any habituation.

Moreover, when adaptation does seem possible, it is difficult to draw a distinction between the effect of learning and physiological tolerance. These results suggest three possible hypotheses.

1. True physiological tolerance to narcosis can occur, but only in certain circumstances and these circumstances are not yet known.

2. Divers may think that they are really adapting to narcosis but, in fact, they are just learning to cope with it.

3. It is possible that divers base their opinions regarding adaptation in large part on their subjective symptoms.

As mentioned earlier, when divers in our experiments were unaware of which gas they were breathing at depth, they were unable to identify it based on subjective symptoms alone. They chose wrongly 80% of the time.

## Conclusions

Narcosis is a condition affecting the physical and mental state of people who breathe air or mixtures containing nitrogen or other inert gases at pressures greater than 4ATA.

The signs and symptoms cover a wide range of severity, from mild impairment of performance to hallucinations and general anaesthesia.

Conventional scuba diving theory holds that narcosis occurs when molecules of a narcotic gas expand the volume of a hydrophobic membrane and observations during general anaesthesia have long supported this lipid theory.

However, recent studies have revealed that nitrogen narcosis is caused instead by interaction with the production, release and uptake of some brain neurotransmitters.

Individual susceptibility to narcosis varies widely but eventually, as depth increases, almost all divers become impaired.

Studies have demonstrated that substituting hydrogen and helium for nitrogen in a diver's breathing mix helps reduce the incidence of narcosis.

Contrary to popular belief, however, external environmental factors have no significant influence on nitrogen narcosis.

Also contrary to popular belief, the effects of nitrogen narcosis can persist for a prolonged period after surfacing.

## Take-home messages

- Nitrogen narcosis may impair a diver's ability to function effectively or even survive.
- Divers are more likely to experience nitrogen narcosis than DCS.
- Nitrogen narcosis alters the higher functions of the nervous system.
- Cerebral impairment persists for at least 30 minutes after surfacing.
- Divers cannot develop tolerance to nitrogen narcosis but they can learn to cope with it.
- Divers may feel less "narked" when they ascend from depth but, objectively, they are still just as "narked".

12

# TECHNICAL DIVING

By: Peter Buzzacott, Miroslav Rozloznik

## Changing the status quo

Diver training in the early days was more physically demanding than it is today. Instructors were frequently ex-military, courses were often taught in a military style and the equipment was basic by today's standards.

Four items of dive equipment, in particular, have dramatically altered the diving community's demography: the submersible pressure gauge (SPG), the buoyancy control device (BCD), the dive computer and the dry suit.

Before the 1970s, analogue SPGs were not widely available and divers relied upon a valve fitted with a lever-tensioned spring to let them know when they were low on air. The spring restricted access to the supply and made it harder for the diver to breathe when the air pressure in the cylinder dropped below a certain level. When divers sensed an increase in breathing resistance, they knew their remaining air supply was low. So they would pull the lever to release the spring and give them access to all the remaining air in the cylinder. Then they could begin their ascent, breathing normally.

There were problems with this mechanical warning system, however. It was easy to knock the lever into the "off" position accidentally while diving, meaning the diver had no reserve air supply when the cylinder ran low and it began to get difficult to breathe.

That's why instructors taught new divers how to deal calmly with out-of-air scenarios.

Today, these reserve valves are now rarely seen and never used, thanks to the universal availability of SPGs. Now, divers can see exactly how much air they have in their cylinders at any point during a dive simply by reading their SPG.

As a diver descends, the increasing water pressure compresses their wetsuit, reducing the water they displace and increasing their negative buoyancy. Before BCDs made an appearance in the late-1970s, divers would weight themselves for a certain planned depth. This meant that they often needed to swim upwards against the downward force exerted by their own negative buoyancy.

Therefore, they had to be fit and instructors would test their fitness, and their resolve, with tasks such as taking the scuba unit off underwater, switching the air off, swimming up to the surface for a breath, and then free-diving back down to the scuba unit, turning on the air and putting it back on again. Known as the "ditch and don", this exercise was essentially a stress test. Negative buoyancy swims became a thing of the past when divers started using BCDs.

Today, divers no longer have to rely on decompression tables. Dive computers automatically adjust the decompression obligation as divers move up and down in the water column.

Over the last two decades, technical diving has developed steadily among more adventurous and committed divers. Technical diving is diving beyond the accepted limits of recreational diving, in an overhead environment such as a cave, a shipwreck or under ice, or with required decompression stops, which place the diver in a virtual overhead environment.

The use of nitrox, blends of oxygen and nitrogen other than air, has become increasingly common and almost all recreational dive computers can now compute nitrox decompression. Some can measure trimix decompression too.

Trimix is a blend of oxygen, nitrogen and helium. In the late 1980s, responding to the needs of explorers such as cave diver Sheck Exley, Dr Bill Hamilton released the first set of trimix dive tables for recreational use.

In 1997, AP Valves in Cornwall, UK produced the Buddy Inspiration, the first successful fully closed-circuit rebreather (CCR) designed for recreational use. Perhaps surprisingly, the concept of rebreathers is actually much older than open-circuit diving but they were previously mostly used by military divers. They were also used by pioneering cavers in order to pass flooded sections of cave known as "sumps".

As soon as these new CCRs became available, images of previously un-dived shipwrecks and caves started appearing in dive magazines. At the same time, within a year, five experienced UK recreational divers died using Buddy Inspirations. Divers were starting *"to boldly go where no man has gone before"*, but not everyone was coming back alive.

The use of helium in the breathing gas, along with deep dives and long decompression procedures, created a demand for better thermal protection and this led to the development of different kinds of dry suits. Nowadays, dry suit divers often also deploy supplementary measures. These may include an active electrical heating system, argon gas for suit insulation or a thermal reflective vest. However, the diver's head still remains relatively poorly insulated.

Technical divers may represent only a minority of the recreational diving community but they spend a disproportionate amount of money pursuing their chosen sport. The equipment costs much more than a standard recreational set-up. Trimix, oxygen for decompression and long boat trips out to sea on boats with fewer customers aboard are all expensive.

Over time, more rebreather manufacturers pitched into the recreational market. Simultaneously, nitrox became available for recreational divers in popular diving destinations such as the Great Barrier Reef and the Red Sea. Divers can now get access to nitrox and, to a lesser extent, trimix and CCR absorbent in many places.

### Turning Tek

Technical diver training was originally only available via specialist agencies, such as IANTD, GUE and TDI. Now, you can also "turn tek" via most of the traditional recreational training associations such as CMAS, SSI and PADI.

The most common first step for a recreational diver wanting to get into technical diving is to learn procedures for planned decompression diving, coupled with strategies to accelerate decompression through the use of nitrox mixtures. The training usually includes procedures for conceivable failures such as losing gas, losing a mask, dive computer failure, torch malfunction and auto-inflation of the BCD or dry suit. Also included are protocols for redundancy and gas management.

Next comes a normoxic trimix course for dives down to 60m (200ft). Normoxic, in this case, may include gases with an oxygen content as low as 18%, which is lower than the oxygen percentage of air at sea level but is still breathable at the surface.

Beyond 60m (200ft), divers must use a bottom mix with a lower fraction of oxygen, for example trimix 10/70, which contains 10% oxygen and 70% helium. A gas containing only 10% oxygen cannot be breathed safely at the surface so the diver needs to carry what is known as a "travel mix" and use this from the surface down to a depth where the "bottom mix" becomes breathable. This travel mix might be a normoxic mix or it could be a hyperoxic mix like nitrox 50, which can be used again on ascent for accelerated decompression.

For example, at the start of the dive the diver breathes nitrox 50, which is safe to breathe down to 20m (66ft). At 10m (33ft), the oxygen partial pressure in the diver's trimix 10/70 bottom mix becomes greater than 0.2 ATM, so the diver can switch to it.

In a cave, where return by the same route is certain, the diver can then cache the nitrox 50 on a line at 20m (66ft) or thereabouts, so it is available as soon as possible during the ascent but cannot accidentally be breathed at a deeper depth where the oxygen level will be toxic.

In an open sea environment, the diver will keep the nitrox 50 cylinder attached to them because there is always a chance that a current may prevent a return along the descent path.

The deeper divers go, the more gas they need and helium is quite expensive, so CCRs are the solution for an increasing number of divers. The helium and other inert gases in the breathing mix are recycled completely, while metabolised oxygen is replaced and carbon dioxide is removed by the chemical absorbent.

Therefore, CCRs offer far greater efficiency of gas usage and are thus more economical for those who dive frequently. However, for the occasional technical diver, the high cost of a rebreather, training, carbon dioxide absorbent and oxygen monitoring sensor cells make open-circuit still a less expensive option.

One form of "tek" involves diving in caves, and the progression from recreational diver to cave diver is now clearly established and standardised by various training agencies.

First, the training takes the diver into caverns to learn the basics of safe cave diving, including the five golden rules concerning gas planning, maximum depth, adequate lighting, marking the exit route and the need for training. New skills introduced at this time include maintaining proper trim (body position) and finning techniques, such as the frog kick, that minimise the risk of stirring up silt and thereby losing sight of the exit path.

After taking a cavern diver course and making some cavern dives to gain enough experience, the next level of training is usually an intermediate phase in which divers start diving with more than one cylinder and practice using reels and lines.

Some caves have a "gold line" from the entrance through the main passage. Others require the team to lay a line themselves. (The lead diver does this.) All lines begin some distance beyond the cave entrance so as not to tempt curious novices into following a line from open water into the cave.

Divers at this training level are usually not permitted to leave the main line to explore side passages or continue into the cave beyond the point where they have used a third of their gas supply (thereby leaving a third for exiting from the cave and a third as a backup or to give to an out-of-air buddy, if required).

Each training agency has different ways of delineating the various levels, but they are all intended to encourage new cave divers to gain experience at one level before moving on to the next.

The final level of basic cave diver training includes learning how to dive complex caves, running short lines called "jumps" and using line markers such as arrows and "cookies". These serve to indicate which divers are still in the cave and also show the direction to the quickest way out.

Each level of diving increases the degree of difficulty and the potential for diver anxiety. The advice divers are always given is; “don’t go too far, too soon”.

There are a few other pathways to becoming a cave diver. In the United Kingdom, for example, divers serve an apprenticeship. Many training agencies offer cavern and cave-diver certifications, and the quality of these depends on the instructor. As is the case with dive courses in general, interested divers should post inquiries on dive forums and visit technical diving websites to find out more. Before signing up for a course, they should try to contact someone who was trained by the instructor they are considering. The value of a patient, sympathetic instructor when you are heading into a place beyond your comfort zone cannot be overstated.

The two pathways to technical diving, the deep path and the cave path, can overlap when divers start penetrating shipwrecks or find a cave that goes deep. As well as the foundation courses, there are specialist courses that cover things like using rebreathers in caves and deploying underwater scooters for long penetrations.

There is no generally accepted medical examination specifically for technical diving. In some European countries, it is enough to just complete a recreational diving medical questionnaire to embark on a technical diving course.

A technical diver must be physically fit, as safe saturation and desaturation require efficient perfusion and diffusion of tissues. The majority of factors involved in diving injuries are diver-related and one area of medical screening that has not been accorded the importance it deserves is the psychological evaluation of technical divers, in particular with regard to their propensity for risk-taking and thrill-seeking.

Attention to detail is a desirable attribute among rebreather divers in particular, where shortcuts, poor maintenance and incomplete pre-dive checks are commonly the cause of diving fatalities.

Dr Bill Oigarden recently studied common personality types in cave diving. He separated cave divers into eight types, based upon their primary diving activities. These types were:

- Exploration Cave Divers

- Technical Cave Divers
- Driven/Passionate Cave Divers
- Lifelong/Lifestyle Cave Divers
- Recreational Cave Divers
- Sump/Cold Water Cave Divers
- Solo Cave Divers, and
- Cave Diving Instructors.

Oigarden found that each type had particular characteristics and considered inherent risks differently. For example, some cave divers might consider travelling extended distances into a complex system acceptable, but not find the prospect of being responsible for trainees in a cave environment appealing at all.

The opposite might be true for an experienced cave diving instructor.

Classifying cave divers in this manner allows a detailed snapshot of the characteristics of certain types of cave diver and how they might view specific risks and potential areas of concern. Comparing different types of cave divers could be a good way to answer the question, "Who do I want to cave dive with?"

## Know the limits

Not every dive computer is designed for planned decompression diving. Many recreational dive computers offer decompression information but they were never supposed to be used for planning decompression dives. These "no decompression" computers are largely untested for decompression diving and should not be relied upon for planning serious decompression dives.

Even dedicated decompression dive computers have their limits.

Here is an extract from David Shaw's website, describing his record dive to 270m (900ft) in Bushmansgat, South Africa.

*"This was not to be a computer dive. I was carrying two VR3s and a Nitek He, but I was only going to be using them as bottom timers. The VR3 algorithm at this depth was not for me. The dive would have been far too long. The Nitek He could not cope with the fact I was diving a rebreather and would be bent in a flash, thus my decision to use VPM-B generated tables. I carried a whole swag of plans on slates."*

Of course, most of us will never go as deep as this and dedicated technical diving computers are more than adequate for the type of diving we do.

The message remains, however: check your dive computer and know its limits.

There is a second important message in David Shaw's last sentence. Contingency planning isn't just for when disaster strikes. It can show divers how an extra few metres or an extra few minutes can change their decompression obligation and/or gas consumption requirements.

On the way up, technical divers need to monitor their ascent rate closely, so technical dive computers should show the time in minutes and seconds instead of just minutes. This helps divers maintain consistent ascent rates.

The principle of redundancy in technical diving extends to all procedures and equipment. Redundant (or parallel) sources of gas, decompression information and lighting are always carried: even sometimes redundant scooters.

In terms of probability, having a redundant system can reduce the risk of fatality due to equipment failure considerably.

For example, if the probability of a total loss of gas from a free-flowing regulator is, for the sake of mathematical simplicity, 1 in 1000 dives, then, if a diver wears two independent cylinders with two independent regulators, both regulators must fail to cause total gas loss.

Therefore, the risk of total gas loss due to equipment failure is 1 in 1,000 dives x 1 in 1000 dives, which makes 1 in 1,000,000 dives.

## The frontier of physiology

Beyond recreational depths, the technical diving community is steadily pushing the frontier of recreational diving towards deeper and less-forgiving environments. Rebreathers are now commonplace in certain regions. Using long-range scooters, technical divers are reaching further and further into caves, often with experimental decompression schedules. These developments carry consequences.

First, the clinical manifestations of DCS are often different after breathing multiple gas blends on the way back up from a depth of 100m (330ft). Inner-ear DCS has become widely reported in the last twenty-five years and is often associated with a PFO. The consensus of medical opinion is that the risk of DCS in recreational divers with a PFO is between 2.5 to 6.5 times greater than in divers without a PFO. The risk remains so small, however, that routine screening for a PFO is still not justified.

In technical diving, however, divers go beyond recreational limits and have to complete multiple decompression stops before surfacing. At least one technical diver training agency recommends divers get screened for a PFO before engaging in dives with required decompression stops.

Rebreathers are typically quite unforgiving if the diver makes an error. Diving with a rebreather requires more exhaustive training, as well as rigorous maintenance and lengthy pre-dive checks. For example, if recreational divers forget to turn their scuba tank valve on they will realise very quickly when they find they can't breathe. They will normally still be in the shallows and be able to surface to have their valve turned on or to reach behind them and turn the valve on themselves. This is an incident, rather than an accident.

But, in the case of rebreather diving, if a diver forgets to turn on their oxygen cylinder, there is no immediate consequence. The oxygen already in the breathing loop is consumed slowly and unnoticeably until the level drops to a point where the diver suddenly loses consciousness.

Death ensues.

This has happened to several rebreather divers.

It is generally accepted that rebreathers carry a much higher risk compared with open-circuit scuba diving, although the exact degree remains unknown. A recent analysis has estimated a factor of between 4-fold and 10-fold. The risk of a fatality while diving on open circuit scuba is thought to be between 0.6 and 2.1 per 100,000 dives.

Another relatively recent development in recreational scuba diving is the ability to begin diving at a younger age. At least one major training agency now offers scuba diving lessons to children from the age of 10, albeit with depth and supervision restrictions. If you look at training agency guidelines, you will find that it is possible to learn how to dive on a rebreather dive when you are as young as 15. Not much is known about the effects of decompression on the physiology of young divers. Research into the effects of diving among children in general continues.

At the other end of the age scale, it is only now that people have been diving recreationally for forty years that we are starting to consider the long-term effects of diving. We know that bubbles often form in our bodies even after dives that are considered safe and that these bubbles cause measurable effects on the cells and function of the endothelium, the inner lining of our blood vessels.

Will a lifetime of deep decompression diving cause memory deterioration or other undesirable late effects? A recent article suggested that there might be very minor changes in the cognitive function of veteran recreational divers, although these may not affect their quality of life. There is also some evidence of this in professional divers, albeit limited.

Meanwhile, scuba diving is here to stay. It is now easier than ever to learn to dive and, thereafter, to progress rapidly to ever-deeper depths. Dive equipment has never been so affordable or so user-friendly. Most modern dive computers will display decompression information for repeated dives well beyond recreational limits.

Before dive computers were common, older divers and medical specialists would assume, for example, that anyone diving to 50m (165ft) would know that they had better not dive again in the afternoon and that it would be wise to allow at least a full day for their body to desaturate before diving again.

However, it is not uncommon these days for divers to show up at hyperbaric chambers with DCS after having made multiple deep dives, one after another.

While the technology has progressed, there is a growing concern that basic diving knowledge is falling to lower and lower levels. Many new divers no longer learn about dive tables and fail to appreciate the relationship between depth and no-stop time or learn the rules for exceptional exposures.

It is unsurprising, therefore, that some divers acquire this knowledge for the first time in a hyperbaric chamber. Even in technical diving courses, it has become more rare to learn dive planning with tables. This means some newly minted technical divers might one day find themselves unsure of what to do when their battery-powered dive computers go flat during a long dive.

## Predictions

We predict that the face-to-face component of diver training will continue to diminish. Over this century the Internet has become so commonplace that diving course students now regularly complete the cognitive development portion of their course online. It is only a matter of time before fully online dive courses become available. Already at least one rebreather manufacturer is offering online certification for their particular model of rebreather, with no face-to-face component at all.

It is also plausible that redundancy of specialised equipment will be more and more common, leading to the development of modular, redundant options. This may encourage technical divers to rely on their equipment even more than they do now.

Of particular concern to old-school technical divers is that the use of dive computers is being adopted as a fail-safe for decompression planning. The marriage of PC-based decompression planning software and diver-worn wrist computers has been welcomed by recreational as well as technical divers but this should not mean the fundamentals of dive planning should be handed over to a computer entirely.

A solid grounding in the theory that underpins the relationship between a diver´s physiology, physical fitness, depth, time, decompression obligations and gas consumption gives a technical diver the ability to spot weaknesses and flaws in computer-based modelling.

While dive computers continue to improve in terms of reliability as well as their approximation of human tolerance for decompression stress, technical divers should still learn table-based dive planning, just as scientists and engineers continued to learn how a slide rule worked when electronic calculators first appeared.

Until computing power matched their demands completely, they felt it was prudent not to abandon the old ways immediately. We are in a transition phase now and not yet quite ready to rely totally on dive computers. One training agency has even taken a stand against using them at all because their success in ensuring safe decompression remains to be scientifically evaluated.

At the same time, there is a worry that technical divers are switching from dive tables to dive computers and web-based gas consumption calculations without learning how to deal with situations when these automated systems fail or give the wrong advice.

This regularly results in divers making technology-driven errors, for example, making several repetitive dives to serious depths, merely because the computer didn't tell them they couldn't, or finding out too late that they do not have enough gas to complete a safe decompression, despite the computer telling them beforehand that they would have enough.

During this transition towards a reliance on technology, it would be wise to keep the old skills sharp. More than one diver has had a total computer failure during deco and had to pull out their trusty wet notes to find a contingency plan to switch to.

Wearing more than one computer does not remove the need for out-of-gas and contingency depth plans. Divers also need to be conscious that decompression from non-standard dives commonly seen in cave diving, such as dives with reverse and yo-yo profiles, is not yet fully understood and current procedures may require review.

Last, as training procedures evolve, technical instructors need to stay abreast of the latest research and technical developments. This can be done by attending conferences, reading technical diving magazines and participating in technical diver forums.

## Conclusions

For the occasional technical diver, the cost of a rebreather, training, carbon dioxide absorbent and oxygen monitoring sensor cells means that open circuit is a less expensive option.

Redundant systems may significantly decrease the risk of fatal accidents due to equipment failure.

While dive computers continue to improve in terms of reliability as well as their approximation of human tolerance for decompression stress, table-based dive planning should remain a staple of technical diver training.

In recent years, the increased availability of breathing gas mixtures, together with the development of specialised diving equipment has allowed more divers than ever before to dive beyond traditional recreational dive limits. Such dives, especially in caves, are often associated with reverse and yo-yo profiles. The long-term impact on diver health of this type of diving is not yet fully understood.

**Take-home messages**

- Technical diver training is now widely available.
- Improved dive equipment has allowed more divers to dive deeper and for longer.
- Divers are exploring new frontiers and new pathologies are likely to appear, requiring new treatments and preventative strategies.
- Decompression planning models have limits and cannot apply equally to all divers, therefore, whenever opportunities arise while diving beyond recreational limits, divers would be wise to err on the side of caution and be extra conservative.
- Soak up technical diving knowledge but be aware that not all of it is accurate. Half of what you have been taught is probably untrue. To borrow from a famous quote about advertising, unfortunately, we do not yet know which half.

- Prudence and conservatism are the watchwords. It is always sad to have to treat bent divers who were not aware of the risk they were taking when embarking on the dive that bent them.

13

# COMMERCIAL DIVING

By: Jean Pierre Imbert, Murat Egi

IT IS IMPORTANT THAT RECREATIONAL DIVERS UNDERSTAND what commercial divers do and the profound differences between the two types of diving in terms of both equipment and procedures. The key difference is that, in commercial diving, surface supervisors control all dives and decompressions: not divers.

## Surface supplied diving

Unlike recreational diving procedures, commercial diving methods are well-defined by regulations, industry guidance and company manuals.

Commercial diving operations include:

1. **Scuba diving,** although this is rare. Scuba diving is banned in North Sea commercial diving operations and most European countries. Scuba divers have a limited gas supply, no communication with the surface, and, in most cases, no safety link to the surface.

2. **Surface-supplied diving**, where divers are supplied from the surface through an umbilical that provides them with gas, audio and video communications, a safety line and a hot water supply for suit heating.

The divers are deployed from a basket. The bottom mix can be air or mixed gas, the decompression mix can be nitrox or pure oxygen. Decompression procedures include in-water decompression or surface decompression in a deck chamber. This is the preferred method.

3. **Wet bell diving**, where divers are deployed in a wet bell with a gas-filled dome. The wet bell provides more comfort and control and permits divers to spend longer in the water.

Wet bells are used for both air and mixed gas diving and, on ascent, divers can decompress using oxygen from a mask from a depth of 12m (40ft) because the environment in which they are sitting is dry.

4. **Bell bounce diving** is diving in a small bell system, designed to be easy to mobilise. The system comprises a two-man bell, a handling frame and a chamber for transfer under pressure (TUP).

Divers can breathe air or mixed gas at the bottom but usually, the chamber is filled with air while they are recovered. They perform pure oxygen breathing sessions on masks at the end of their decompression.

Small bell systems can support bounce diving down to 120m (400ft) and bottom times of up to 2 hours.

5. **Saturation diving**, where the divers are kept under pressure at the surface and deployed underwater from a diving bell.

## Medical fitness to dive

Authorised physicians assess the medical fitness of commercial divers according to government guidelines. The fitness standards for commercial divers are much higher than those cited in the health declarations required by recreational diving organisations. For commercial divers, there may be restrictions on body fat content and visual, auditory and cardiopulmonary functions. The European Diving Technology Committee has recently been attempting to harmonise fitness standards for commercial divers across Europe.

## A dive team

In commercial diving, a diver is normally alone in the water but has a lot of topside "buddies". A team of a minimum of four people is required for a commercial dive:

- one diver,
- one supervisor,
- one dive tender and
- one standby diver.

Secure hardwired communication between the diver and the supervisor is compulsory. Signals via the lifeline to the dive tender are used as a backup in case the hardwired communication system fails. The supervisor must document everything. There is no buddy check system. It is the supervisor who checks each diver and sends them off on the diving operation.

Commercial divers do not decide on their dive profile. Most of the time they are guided by the supervisor who reads the diver's depth from a pneumogauge on the diver control panel.

### The control panel and the pneumogauge

The control panel for mixed gas or saturation diving can be very complicated but a simple portable unit is usually enough for onshore diving. The main component is the pneumogauge and the panel should allow the use of multiple gas supplies.

At least two gas sources are necessary to enable continuous operation by switching from one to the other.

The emergency scuba tank and the regulator first stage carried by the diver to feed the band mask or the helmet is not counted as either the primary or secondary gas source. If a diver has to switch to emergency scuba the dive is aborted.

The umbilical of a commercial diver consists of at least 3 components:

- a gas supply hose,
- a communication cable and
- a hollow tube called the pneumogauge hose.

The usual accuracy of an analogue gauge is about 3%. Dive computers have an accuracy of about ±5cm. The accuracy of a pneumogauge is very high and it needs to be calibrated at regular intervals.

In spite of this, according to US Navy procedures, dive supervisors should not apply their decompression tables to the actual depth reading. They must add an additional depth factor. For instance, if the depth reading is 63m (210ft), dive supervisors will add 1.2m (4ft) and look up the decompression requirement for 64.2m (214ft) in their tables.

## Decompression mode

Diving beyond no-decompression stop limits is acceptable in commercial diving. It is the supervisor's responsibility to choose how the diver will decompress. There are four ways to decompress:

- in-water decompression,
- surface decompression,
- bell bounce and
- saturation.

In-water decompression is used mostly on shallow, relatively warm dives onshore and in confined water for projects such as harbour construction.

Surface decompression is also used extensively in onshore diving. Time, equipment and operational costs are too high for divers to spend a long time in the water doing decompression stops. Sometimes environmental factors such as waves and water temperature limit how long divers can stay at shallow decompression stops.

Surface decompression procedures require an on-site hyperbaric chamber. When surface decompression is carried out, the diver follows all the in-water decompression stops up to a certain depth, 12m (40ft) according to US Navy procedures or 9m (30ft) if following DCIEM procedures.

Then the diver rushes to the surface and continues their decompression in the onsite chamber. It is a challenge for the diver and the surface team members to undress divers and pressurize them back down to 12m (40ft) within 5 minutes of surfacing (7 minutes if following DCIEM procedures). Any delay is compensated for by switching to a treatment table.

The third and fourth decompression methods are widely used in offshore diving. Saturation and bell bounce diving decompression methods are very different from recreational diving and are described in the next sections.

## The history of saturation diving

The history of offshore commercial diving is intertwined with the development of North Sea oil and gas production. In the early 1960s, it was suspected that gas fields found in Holland could continue under the North Sea and the first drilling contracts were awarded to famous rigs like Ocean Viking. The Gulf Tide jack-up discovered the 1.6-billion-barrel reservoir of Ekofisk just before Christmas Eve 1969, a nice gift for Phillips. More discoveries followed and, in 1971, Shell hit the jackpot with the discovery of the Brent field between the Shetlands and Norway.

The development of the North Sea oil fields led to the development of offshore commercial diving. In less than 20 years, from the early 1970s, the time of the pioneers, to the 1990s, diving companies designed equipment, trained personnel, created procedures and built a new industry with an impressive track record.

In the beginning, everything had to be invented. The initial expertise came from Naval units, which were the only organisations with standards and formally trained personnel. They brought with them a tough work discipline that persists to this day on board Diving Support Vessels (DSV). They imposed their jargon, such as "Roger Roger," which can be heard in dive control centres all over the world.

The second source of expertise was divers from the Gulf of Mexico, who flew over to Aberdeen in Scotland attracted by the very high wages. Famous for their thick belt buckles, Texan boots and Ray-Ban sunglasses, they introduced the fibreglass Superlite helmet from Bev Morgan, the hot water suit from DUI and silver duct tape: three major pieces of equipment without which offshore diving would never have taken off the way it did.

They also brought over the US Navy Diving Manual, the only set of diving procedures available at the time, and this became the offshore diver's Bible. Today, you can still see the influence of US Navy culture in commercial diving operations.

As Europe was seeking energy independence through North Sea oil and gas, research and development money started flowing in and during the "twenty glory years", the European Economic Community supported technical development in the commercial diving industry.

One of the many challenges was to develop saturation diving procedures for divers to work between 100m (330ft) and 180m (570ft): the standard North Sea bottom depths.

Compared with other forms of diving, the development of saturation diving is relatively recent. The concept for the decompression phase was already available when Haldane published his work in 1908. Davies had already designed a simple bell system for bounce diving.

However, there was simply no need for saturation diving, not even for tunnel work. It was Dr Behnke, from the US Navy, who first formulated the idea after the recovery of the crew of the USS Squalus in 1942. Thereafter, major progress was made in both the USA and France.

In the late 1950s. Dr George Bond carried out key animal experiments, and then, in the early 1960s, Jacques Cousteau ran the Conshelf (Pre-Continent) experiments while Ed Link operated the Man-in-the-Sea habitats. Soon after, in 1964, the US Navy started the Sealab series of habitat saturations. This programme was later continued by NASA under the name Tektite.

In 1967 Professor Chouteau and Cousteau carried out Pre-Continent III to 150m (500ft). This experiment was unique in that an oil well head was sunk near the habitat so that divers could run practical experiments.

The first commercial diving saturation was carried out in 1965 on the Smith Mountain Dam in Virginia by the Westinghouse Electric Corporation Undersea Division under the direction of Jerry O'Neill. The system consisted of a large Deck Decompression Chamber (DDC) and a Personnel Transfer Capsule (PTC), which could be mated to the DDC under pressure.

Similar commercial diving systems would soon spread across the world. In 1969, COMEX carried out a saturation operation to 200m (660ft) in the Gulf of Biscayne for the Institut Français du Pétrole (IFP), a state enterprise. Five years later the huge concrete platform of Brent Bravo was installed.

### Saturation diving concepts

Saturation diving is a technique whereby divers live under pressure in a chamber on board a ship and are deployed underwater from the chamber in a diving bell. The pressure they live at in the chamber is referred to as their "storage depth".

The divers work at depths of 10 to 20m (33 to 66ft) above or below their storage depth, and their working dives are referred to as "excursions". During any single excursion, they can move up and down within their working depth limits. Their storage depth can be adjusted by pressurisation or depressurisation, allowing them to work at different depths. Generally, several teams of divers are saturated together in the chamber and this permits continuous operations at depth. At the end of a work period, the whole team transfers to a separate chamber that is gradually decompressed "to the surface".

The average rate of ascent "to the surface" is around 30m (100ft) per day, so, on a standard North Sea project, it takes 4 to 5 days to get the divers back to normal atmospheric pressure.

The importance of saturation diving in the North Sea grew over time. During the early development phase, the work consisted mainly of short interventions from time to time on the wellhead. These contracts were conducted with bell bounce diving.

During the following construction phase, all the work took place on the sea bed and was therefore carried out exclusively with saturation diving. Beginning in 1982, inspection and repair jobs began to be awarded for the maintenance of various installations. Most of these jobs were shallow and could be performed by divers on air. This prompted a new interest in air tables.

Today, the North Sea market is split: 20% of the work involves shallow air surface-supplied interventions and 80%

is heliox saturation diving. It is estimated that, on average, 1000 saturation exposures are made each year in the North Sea.

Excursion dives allow divers to perform work from a given storage depth. The concept was first publicised by Alan Krasberg following the initial Westinghouse saturation operations. At the time he claimed an impressive track record of 33 saturations.

Bornmann adapted Workman's M-values to create early US Navy helium-oxygen saturation excursion tables, treating excursion dives as no-decompression bounce dives performed from a saturation depth.

For example, from a 90m (300ft) saturation depth, a descending excursion of 30m (100ft) to a depth of 120m (400ft) for 100 minutes would require a diver to do no decompression stops when returning to the initial storage depth.

The tables were tested by Summitt at the Navy Experimental Diving Unit (NEDU) in 1969. In his validation studies, no DCS was observed following 1126 excursions from 15m (50ft) to 45m (150ft) deeper than saturation depths ranging from 45m (150ft) to 180m (570ft).

Taking into account other sources, particularly the work of Barnard from the British Royal Navy, the US Navy continued to work on saturation excursion tables.

Exhaustive studies were performed between February 1974 and June 1976 at the NEDU, which was then located in Washington DC, and these subsequently served as the basis for the current US Navy excursion tables and ascent procedures, first published in the 1984 revision of the US Navy Manual.

### US Navy saturation decompression procedures

The 1984 US Navy saturation decompression procedures are the classic reference.

They are characterised by:

- 1. A relatively moderate $ppO_2$ in the decompression chamber (350 to 400 mbar, 35 to 40 kPa),
- 2. Varying rates of ascent, a feature left over from the many attempts by the US Navy over the years to make final decompression safer.
- 3. Relatively slow decompression rates, linked to the low chamber $ppO_2$.
- 4. Stops during each night from 00h to 06h and in the afternoon from 14h to 16h, resulting in a total hold time of 8 hours a day.
- 5. A controlled chamber oxygen percentage lower than 22% in the last few metres of the ascent to reduce the risk of fire.
- 6. The final decompression starting immediately after the divers have returned from an excursion dive to the storage depth, except if this was an upward excursion.

### COMEX saturation decompression procedures

Some diving companies conducted independent research programmes and came up with their own procedures. The initial COMEX heliox saturation regulations were designed by Dr Xavier Fructus based on early experiments performed at the Marseilles Hyperbaric Centre.

These were characterised by:

- 1. High $ppO_2$ during decompression (600 mbar or even 800 mbar, 60 kPa and 80 kPa) and more rapid ascent rates.
- 2. Continuous decompression with no night stop, and
- 3. Flexible excursion procedures.

**Norwegian saturation decompression procedures**

In the later period of North Sea development, government authorities were concerned about decompression safety and the use of shorter decompressions for commercial advantage.

Dr Val Hempleman was contracted by the British Admiralty to evaluate the various saturation procedures in use and, in 1988, the Norwegian Petroleum Directorate (NPD) organized an international conference dedicated to saturation decompression safety.

Finally, in 1990, the NPD initiated a study aiming at the harmonization of saturation procedures in the Norwegian sector.

The project was split into two phases.

The first phase was used to record practices employed by the five diving contractors operating in the Norwegian sector.

The second phase set a common framework for saturation diving down to 180m (570ft). This resulted in the publication of the NORSOK U100 standard for manned underwater intervention in 1999. The NORSOK procedures seemed to be something of a compromise. One can recognise bits from each contributor, including, indirectly, from the old US Navy manual.

However, these standardised procedures have been used since 1999 in the Norwegian sector and the overall result is a very conservative decompression protocol.

### Brazilian saturation decompression procedures

When saturation diving started in Brazil at the turn of the 1980s, there was no comprehensive Brazilian state legislation, so the rules applied were derived from the diving manuals of the companies operating in the area. These were COMEX (now Acergy) and Marsat (now Fugro). State legislation, which was closely related to UK regulations, was eventually published in 1988. Later, in 2004, the Brazilian authorities imposed national procedures that were derived from COMEX's deep saturation strategies.

### Current saturation procedures

The current commercial diving market is split between three major subsea contractors, Technip, Acergy and Subsea 7, a dozen second-level players with international scope and multiple smaller companies that mostly concentrate on coastal or inland work.

Diving procedures in use on board saturation Dive Support Vessels (DSVs) can be classified into three categories:

- 1. Saturation instructions derived from US Navy procedures: the main adaptation being to increase chamber $ppO_2$ to 500mbar (50kPa).
- 2. Saturation procedures independently developed by the individual company.
- 3. National saturation instructions imposed by government agencies such as in Norway and Brazil.

There is now an international harmonisation of the oxygen protocol for final chamber decompression. All the protocols use a constant chamber $ppO_2$ of 500mbar (50kPa) from the start of the decompression up to 15m (50ft), and a chamber oxygen percentage of between 22% and 23% (kept low because of fire risk) from 15m (50ft) to the surface.

### Safety assessment of current saturation procedures

Assessment of the safety performance of diving procedures is part of all company safety management systems, however, this information is kept confidential for reasons that are unclear. Thus there is little information available to evaluate the present level of safety in terms of saturation decompression performance or to compare saturation procedures between companies.

Safety performance comparisons require statistical techniques. The safety of a diving procedure is measured by the DCS rate. Generally, companies know the numerator, as incidents must be reported to government authorities and dedicated forms are included in the company reporting system. The main difficulty, as with all diving data analysis, is the denominator. These days diving companies no longer maintain diving databases so there is no information on diver exposures.

DCS symptoms include a wide span of problems, which for operational reasons have long been classified into two categories, Type I and Type II, according to the US Navy Diving Manual.

Type I includes simple symptoms like skin rash or articular or muscle pain. Because the symptoms are obvious, they are reported early and the treatment is initiated without hesitation. In most cases, administration of hyperbaric oxygen and a 10 to 20m (33 to 66ft) recompression will rapidly resolve the symptoms.

Type II DCS is more serious because it affects either the respiratory or the neurological systems. The symptoms are often vague and may include fatigue, headache or general malaise, so diagnosis may be difficult at an early stage or in mild cases. The treatment is complex and requires deep recompression, significant periods of hyperbaric oxygen breathing and fluid intake.

The safety of decompression tables can be defined in terms of the risk of DCS occurrence per dive exposure but a distinction must be made between the two types of symptoms. Final decompression from saturation has always been exclusively associated with Type I (pain only) DCS. Neurological symptoms have been reported by divers immediately upon returning from an excursion bell dive, but the slow rates of saturation decompression have only ever produced articular pain during or after decompression. This makes saturation decompression safety easier to study.

### US Navy saturation safety performance

Several US Navy publications have attempted to evaluate the safety performance of US Navy saturation procedures and excursion tables. A series of tests published in 1976 by Dr Spaur quoted Type I cases during or after final decompression and Type II cases after deep excursions. The following incidence rates were calculated:

a. 1.7 (± 0.8)% for saturation shallower than 90m (300ft).

b. 11.7 (± 6.4) % for saturation deeper than 90m (300ft).

Another study by Dr Berghage indicated an overall DCS incidence of 2.6% over 265 man exposures.

These data explain why, although many diving contractors still claim to use the original US Navy procedures, most have introduced empirical modifications to improve decompression safety, such as higher oxygen levels in decompression and reduced excursion distances. Even though the US Navy saturation procedures are still considered to be the reference, this is more because their use represents an advantage in terms of an employer's liability than because they correspond to the state of the art and best practice. This is no longer the case.

## Commercial diving databases

In the history of saturation diving, there have been several attempts to set up databases to assess the safety of diving procedures and document the long-term effects of diver exposures.

A symposium on diving databases was organised In Amsterdam in August 1990. The various databases identified were:

1. The HSE database, set up by the British Health and Safety Executive to monitor the safety of air diving in the North Sea UK sector. The system was run by Dr Tom Shield from the National Hyperbaric Centre in Aberdeen. The conclusions of the study were reported in 1986 and were used by the HSE to limit diving exposures in offshore air diving operations.

2. The Hades register that was developed by Seaway and ran until 1994. It covered saturation diving and was used by Seaway to improve its saturation procedures. Data published

from the Hades database indicated an average DCS incidence of 0.5% in saturation diving.

3. The COMEX database. This database was set up in 1974 and was run until approximately 1995. It was published scientifically and used by COMEX for safety assessments, insurance negotiations and claims. COMEX claimed an overall DCS rate of 1% for its operations during the 1980s. For subsequent operations in the 1990s up to 1994, the incidence was only 0.5%.

Unfortunately, these databases are no longer maintained. Anecdotal information suggests that the current level of DCS incidence in commercial saturation diving is around 0.2% (two cases of DCS for every 1000 dives).

Saturation diving is evidently very safe.

## Conclusions

As always, everything was difficult before it became easy. It took 20 years for the offshore industry to develop safe saturation procedures but nowadays the knowledge has spread and the information required to run saturation operations may not take up more than two pages in a company's diving manual.

However, this knowledge is more empirical than theoretical, especially because after 1995 the offshore industry went into a downturn. At that time, research and development were frozen. As a consequence, diving procedures have not evolved since then, although much has been discovered and published in the field of decompression research.

Saturation diving is a good example of successful empirical development but it is time now to revisit existing decompression procedures in light of new scientific knowledge to prepare the next wave of procedures. These may not necessarily be safer, but they may be more flexible.

### Take-home messages

- There is a profound difference, in terms of both equipment and procedures, between recreational and commercial diving. Technical possibilities in commercial diving allow for much longer decompressions controlled by supervisors, rather than divers.
- Commercial diving procedures are a good example of successful empirical development.

# Part Two

# APPENDICES

**Food for Thought 1 to 6** – a series of short essays by the authors of The Science of Diving, exploring ideas related to the material in this book.

**Glossary**

**Acronyms**

**Author / Editor: Scuba Physiological**

**The Original Authors of The Science of Diving**

**References and further reading**

# FOOD FOR THOUGHT 1

## Can we "BAYES" our approach to decompression?

In 1948, Ernst G. Straus said: *"This is so simple God could not have passed it up."* This is a good way of describing the Bayes theorem, a very old formula developed in 1748 by Thomas Bayes, an English Presbyterian Pastor, and refined by Pierre-Simon Laplace thirty years later.

The Bayes theorem is so simple that anyone can grasp the fundamentals behind it. 30,000 papers have been published based on it, including many within the field of medical science. According to an Internet search, using *Bayes* and *Bayesian* as keywords, we found that, in a 4-year period, about 1000 medical papers using this approach are published, slightly more than one for every working day.

In the era of increasingly large diving-related databases, be they military, commercial or recreational, one might reasonably expect a lot of papers published in the diving field to be based on Bayesian principles. However, when we did a search using the Bayes keywords and adding "scuba diving", we were rather disappointed to find just two papers.

At its simplest, the Bayesian model can be expressed as condition 1 plus condition 2 leads to condition 3. These "conditions" are factors for which the subject (diver or patient) is positive and which are identified from a large set of candidate parameters. When applied to large databases, the approach has the advantage of determining the probability of particular associations using very large numbers of subjects, even when relatively little is known about individuals.

These associative rules are designed to generate a hierarchical approach such as dyspepsia plus epigastric pain leading to heartburn.

This is a conditional statement indicating that dyspepsia and epigastric pain are commonly followed by heartburn. This concept is of considerable interest in our field. A possible association could be scuba diving plus bubbles lead to DCS.

If only it were that simple! It might work that way if our sole purpose was simply to identify cases where DCS was definitively diagnosed. However, in the real world, it has been repeatedly demonstrated that we cannot define a clear-cut relationship between bubbles and DCS. Individuals appear to react in very different ways to decompression stress. Some cope with it very successfully, others less so.

Applying a Bayesian approach, we must consider the number of bubbles (in terms of the number of circulating gas emboli or volume of gas) associated with other factors. For example, we might propose: dive profile plus individual parameters lead to decompression stress.

This approach might work. Can we resolve the dilemma of whether we should focus our studies on decompression stress or DCS?

According to Einstein, yes we can, by applying the simple equation, “A plus B lead to C”, where C stands for a successful life; A stands for enthusiasm and B is the ability to keep one’s mouth shut. Even if this may seem a bit juvenile, it is nevertheless a pearl of wisdom, since enthusiasm is generally in opposition to a strategy of remaining tight-lipped.

Balance is the key. We should not be too exclusive in our approaches to decompression. The Bayes formula shows that there is value in studying both DCS and decompression stress (with or without DCS). In a Bayesian world, two probabilistic approaches have a greater chance of leading to a final third one. That’s what we want!

# FOOD FOR THOUGHT 2

## The oxygen window in decompression

The term "oxygen window" was first used by Behnke in the 1960s but the phenomenon itself had been described much earlier and was known under different names such as "partial pressure vacancy" (Momsen), "partial pressure vacuum" (Sass) or "inherent unsaturation" (Hills).

Unlike nitrogen and helium, oxygen is a metabolic gas. So there is a difference between the oxygen partial pressure in the arterial blood and the venous blood. This difference is referred to as the oxygen window.

Oxygen is consumed by the cells to generate energy, therefore blood leaving the tissues has a lower partial pressure of oxygen than blood entering the tissues. $CO_2$ is produced roughly in equal measure to the consumption of oxygen, however, $CO_2$ is much more soluble in blood than oxygen is. Whereas most of the oxygen (98%) is carried by haemoglobin, $CO_2$ is transported in three ways. About 5-7% is directly dissolved in the plasma and about 10% is bound to haemoglobin and plasma proteins. The rest combines with water to form bicarbonate (HCO3) and $H^+$ atoms.

When it does this, it does not exert hydrostatic pressure as it would in the dissolved gas phase, because the gas atoms or molecules are not free to move about. For a given quantity of oxygen consumed in the metabolism of the tissues, the partial pressure of oxygen (pO2) in the blood will drop from 95 mmHg in the arterial blood to 45 mmHg in the venous blood, whereas the partial pressure of $CO_2$ only rises by 5 mmHg (from 40 to 45 mmHg.)

The net effect of this is a difference of about 45 mmHg in the sum of gas partial pressures between the arterial and venous blood. This happens in normal metabolism, not only in diving situations. The $pO_2$ decreases from the capillary blood vessel to the cells, but the $pCO_2$ does not change very much because of the much higher solubility of $CO_2$. Therefore, the oxygen window is greater in the tissues.

When you breathe oxygen at higher pressures, something strange happens, and this has to do with the binding properties of haemoglobin. Haemoglobin carries oxygen, releasing it into the blood when the blood $pO_2$ drops below a certain threshold. When the blood $pO_2$ is higher than 100 mmHg, no oxygen is released and haemoglobin saturation does not change.

So, the oxygen window is larger (both between arterial blood and the tissues and between the tissues and venous blood) when you dive with higher partial pressures of oxygen.

What does this mean for divers?

Inert gas elimination is not influenced by the presence of other gases in the blood, so a smaller or larger oxygen window does not decrease or increase nitrogen desaturation.

However, once nitrogen bubbles have formed, they slow down further inert gas desaturation. They also possibly provoke DCS. With a higher oxygen partial pressure in the arterial blood, there is consequently less inert gas than when you are breathing air and more of the nitrogen will dissolve in the blood as it comes out of the tissues.

This increases inert gas washout at deeper depths, reduces inert gas supersaturation (as more gas can be dissolved at greater pressures) and reduces the risk of inert gas bubbles forming.

Also, if bubbles do form, the larger oxygen window "opens up" inert gas space in the blood and the tissues. The nitrogen inside a bubble can therefore be "sucked back" into the surrounding blood or tissue, thereby decreasing the bubble's volume. If the oxygen partial pressure is maintained at a high enough level and for long enough, dissolved nitrogen can move to the plasma and be exhaled by the lungs.

Oxygen is a very efficient way to increase inert gas washout, but, when it is used for decompression, other factors need to be taken into account too. It is worth remembering that, in high doses, oxygen is poisonous and both central nervous system and pulmonary oxygen are real threats.

Oxygen can be used at much higher pressures in recompression therapy than when diving, but therapeutic effectiveness still has to be balanced against oxygen toxicity risk.

# FOOD FOR THOUGHT 3

## Just say "NO" to decompression stress

Vascular gas emboli (VGE) start forming during the degassing of tissues in the ascent phase of a dive when bubble precursors called micronuclei grow into bubbles. The precise mechanism of the formation of these micronuclei is still a matter of debate, but they are thought to occur in facilitating regions with surfactants, hydrophobic surfaces or crevices. Different people will produce different quantities of VGE on the same dive.

Subjects in good physical condition have a lower risk of VGE and DCS post-dive. More surprisingly, VGE production may be reduced just with a single pre-dive preconditioning intervention. Studies in rats have shown that a single bout of exercise 20 hours before a dive can reduce post-dive VGE. There is debate over the role of exercise in humans. Depending on its timing and intensity it may increase or decrease bubbles.

We don't know what the precise link is between VGE and the endothelial dysfunction that has been observed post-dive. It has been suggested that a nitric oxide-(NO)-mediated change in the surface properties of the vascular endothelium favours the elimination of gas micronuclei. NO synthase activity increases following 45 minutes of exercise and NO administration immediately before a dive reduces VGE. Nevertheless, bubble production is increased by an NO blockade in sedentary but not in exercised rats, suggesting other biochemical pathways. Factors such as heat-sensitive proteins, antioxidant defences or blood rheology may be involved.

The first link between NO and protection from DCS was detected by chance. In an experiment involving explosive decompression of sedentary rats, resulting in a >80% mortality, some additional rats were needed to complete the experiment but there were no more sedentary rats available, only treadmill-exercised rats. After the decompression, 80% of the running rats survived. The explanation given for this observation was that the presence of NO in the trained rats resulted in fewer bubbles and less DCS.

However, a French study showed that human volunteers had fewer bubbles post-dive after a treadmill exercise than after a cycle-ergometer test. If bubble production was purely related to NO production, the number of bubbles should have been more or less the same in both groups, so where did the difference lie? There are some mechanical differences between the two forms of exercise. During a treadmill test, there is more impact and vibration. It is now hypothesized that micronuclei may also be reduced by mechanical means. This was demonstrated by an experiment in which passive whole-body vibration was applied before diving. This reduced VGE on decompression considerably.

In conclusion, the last word has not yet been spoken concerning the link between NO and a reduction in post-decompression VGE. Studies should be focussed more on high-intensity training, as the reduction of decompression stress after aerobic effort has already been extensively studied. This will allow more understanding of the subtle mechanisms that may protect individuals from DCS. The variable effect of oxygen on bubble decay, with a transient increase of volume in some cases, also requires further investigation.

# FOOD FOR THOUGHT 4

## Hydrophobicity, the link between bubbles, bubblers & autoimmunity

Scientific data suggest that divers can be divided into two different groups: "bubblers" and "non-bubblers". Why this is so cannot be explained by any generally accepted hypothesis.

Some years ago, in experiments on sheep, Hills found evidence of hydrophobicity on the surface of blood vessels. He attributed the hydrophobicity to the presence of phospholipids and suggested that lung surfactant deposits created a hydrophobic lining.

Later, Arieli and Marmur found that there are clearly defined areas on the surface of blood vessels that could be hydrophobic spots, where bubbles nucleate and grow after decompression from higher pressure. They also showed that nanobubbles form spontaneously when a smooth hydrophobic surface is submerged in water containing dissolved gas. It could therefore be that a permanent layer of nanobubbles covers these hydrophobic spots on blood vessels.

The chain of amino acids in a protein may include hydrophobic acids. Gases are attracted to these and reactions take place, altering the proteins' configuration and changing their immunochemical properties. We have seen this happening with bubbles in the blood.

At various times, large protein molecules are carried in the blood. When one of these molecules has a hydrophobic area and comes into contact with the strongly hydrophobic nanobubble layer at a surfactant spot on the endothelium, it sticks to the spot and is detected as a foreign molecule. This sets in motion an autoimmune response.

Just as DCS risk increases with age, so does autoimmune pathology. If hydrophobic active spots increase in area and number with a person's age, this could explain the increase in DCS risk in older people.

The varied incidence of hydrophobic spots in humans may also explain why people vary in sensitivity to autoimmune diseases and to decompression stress: that is, why there are bubblers and non-bubblers.

It may explain too why preconditioning before diving, either by mechanical means such as vibration or by oxygen breathing, thermal energy or physical effort, reduces bubble production.

# FOOD FOR THOUGHT 5

## Is your state... steady?

For many years, diving and hyperbaric medicine have worked to increase our understanding of the effects of environmental stressors on humans. It has demonstrated the importance of oxygen and has taught us not to fear this oxidative molecule, even though the word "oxygen" comes from *occidere,* the Latin word for "to kill".

The scientific literature contains many interesting reports on the potential benefits of supplemental oxygen but there are also reports that include warnings such as, "*the benefits of supplemental oxygen are not yet confirmed, and new findings suggest that potential side-effects should be considered if the inspired oxygen concentration is increased above what is needed to maintain normal arterial oxygen saturation*".

This demonstrates how opinion is divided and how hyperoxic (not necessarily hyperbaric) and hypoxic states can be interpreted. Some have compared oxygen to the lead character in "Dr. Jekyll and Mr. Hyde" but it would be better to think of oxygen as a multifaceted molecule, not just one with a good side and a bad side.

Newer technologies and the speed of modern instrumentation allow us to understand the versatility of oxygen in new and better ways. The environmental sciences are probably the leaders in this field, as their approach is often based on analysing "coping reaction" and speed of adaptation to various stressors. An excellent example, described recently by an Israeli group, is that even old neurological lesions seem to respond in a favourable way to "*oscillations*" of the partial pressure of oxygen. This is an outcome you would not expect.

"Oscillations", "pulsed", "variations" and "acute exposures" are all terms used in the literature to characterize unsteady or transient states. We have been studying steady-state pathophysiology for around 200 years. However, in future, it seems we will face new paradigms that are probably less easy to understand, but will open new frontiers. It seems like oxygen is more of a "slasher" than a two or even three-faced entity. "Slasher" was a term coined by Marci Alboher to describe the growing number of people who cannot give a single-word answer to the question "what do you do for a living?", but instead answer along the lines of music teacher/webmaster/personal trainer etc. Oxygen is clearly a multifaceted actor. This, on the one hand, causes it to be viewed in many different ways. On the other hand, it offers many new avenues for research.

# FOOD FOR THOUGHT 6

## Creativity in science

All scientists attend congresses and listen to presentations. Many are very boring. Happily, others are funny or inspiring, or both. Every paper should be interesting but humour is important too. And, if an interesting message can be concealed within the humour, so much the better. Here are a few examples.

A 5-year-old Canadian boy, Antoine-Olivier Cyr, became the youngest author ever to appear in Pubmed when, with the help of his 8-year-old brother (and his 50-year-old father, a professor of medicine) he produced a very creative article. The piece investigated why Tintin, the hero boy reporter, does not seem to age or, for that matter, mature sexually. After careful analysis, the authors concluded that this was probably due to too many blows to the head, with several episodes of loss of consciousness, leading to hypogonadism and a hypophyseal hormone deficiency.

To reach their hypothesis, the authors counted the total number of instances of head trauma that Tintin endured over his long career as an adventurer and the total number of frames in every Tintin book where Tintin was shown unconscious. Consecutive frames were counted as the time spent unconscious and the number of flying sparrows around Tintin's head indicating the severity of the trauma. All those parameters were then compared to modern trauma scales, with the conclusion that an acquired hormonal deficiency was very likely.

Scientific journals have a long tradition of publishing formal comment-and-reply papers, in which a group of researchers reviews a recently published paper and the authors of the paper respond. Usually, there is substantial disagreement, which is never fully settled. The debate surrounding a 1963 Journal of Geology paper about sediment accumulation rates was a bit different. In this case, the review neither took issue with the results nor even the implications of the paper. It merely pointed out a minor error in the presentation.

*"It is obvious that this error in presenting sedimentation rates has no [effect] whatever on the ages given in the paper. Therefore, the main body of the paper and the conclusions reached require no modification."*

To which the authors replied:

*"Oh well; nobody is perfect".*

Another humorous classic is the well-known paper on the unsuccessful self-treatment of writer's block. This research received independent confirmation only recently (in 2007). The best part of the first paper is one reviewer's answer:

*"I have studied this manuscript very carefully with lemon juice and X-rays and have not detected a single flaw in either design or*

*writing style. I suggest it be published without revision. Clearly, it is the most concise manuscript I have ever seen, yet it contains sufficient detail to allow other investigators to replicate Dr. Upper's failure. In comparison with the other manuscripts I get from you containing all that complicated detail, this one was a pleasure to examine. Surely we can find a place for this paper in the Journal, perhaps on the edge of a blank page."*

At The Future of Diving: 100 Years of Haldane and Beyond meeting in Trondheim in 2009, held in honour of Professor Alf Brubakk on his retirement, one inspiring paper discussed the patterns and rules that can be derived from an in-depth analysis of jazz improvisation. Briefly, the 7 commandments of Jazz improvisation could be summarised as: -

- Provocative competence (deliberate efforts to interrupt habitual patterns)
- Embracing errors as a source of learning
- Shared orientation towards minimal structures that allow maximum flexibility
- Distribution of tasks (continual negotiation and dialogue towards dynamic synchronisation)
- Reliance on retrospective sense-making
- Hanging out with fellow musicians
- Taking turns in soloing and accompanying

This is an inspiring and appealing recipe for science as well as creative production. One does not even need to be a musician to apply the principles of the rules of jazz. So, here is a message for young scientists. A high level of creativity makes science interesting AND fun. Best of all: you do not need to be a great scientist to be part of great science. What are you waiting for? Plunge in!

# GLOSSARY

**Acute**: a medical problem of short duration is described as acute. It is the opposite of chronic, (see below) which denotes long-lasting disease.

**Adiposity**: Fat

**Ambient pressure**: The ambient pressure on an object is the pressure of the surrounding medium, such as a gas or a liquid, that is in contact with the object.

**Angiotensin**: a hormone that causes vasoconstriction and a subsequent increase in blood pressure.

**Apical**: from the top (the adjective of apex)

**Arterial System** (see **Venous system-arterial system** below)

**Atherosclerosis**: hardening and loss of elasticity of medium or large arteries.

**Atomic-force microscopy**: a type of microscopy with very high resolution to the order of fractions of a nanometre.

**Atorvastatin**: a member of the drug class known as statins, which are used primarily as a lipid-lowering agent for the prevention of cardiovascular disease.

**Basal ganglia**: a group of subcortical nuclei in the brain, associated with a variety of functions including control of voluntary motor movements, procedural learning, routine behaviour and habits.

**Bilayer**: a double layer of closely packed atoms or molecules.

**Biophysical**: pertaining to biological physics, an interdisciplinary science that applies the approaches and methods of physics to study biological systems.

**Blood extravasation**: the leakage of blood from a vessel into tissues surrounding it.

**Brachial artery**: the major blood vessel of the upper arm.

**Cavitation**: the formation of vapour cavities in a liquid, small liquid-free zones, bubbles or voids, that are the consequence of forces acting upon the liquid. It usually occurs when a liquid is subjected to rapid changes in pressure that cause the formation of cavities in the liquid where the pressure is relatively low.

**Chronic**: A long-lasting disease is described as chronic. In medicine, chronic is the opposite of acute (see above.)

**COMEX**: Compagnie Maritime d'Expertises - a French undersea engineering company

**Cortical arousal**: the physiological and psychological state of being awoken or of sense organs stimulated to a point of perception, leading to increased heart rate and blood pressure and a condition of sensory alertness, mobility, and readiness to respond.

**Decompression**: The decompression of a diver is the reduction in ambient pressure experienced during ascent from depth. It is also the process of elimination of dissolved inert gases from the diver's body, which occurs during the ascent, during pauses in the ascent known as decompression stops, and after surfacing until gas concentrations reach equilibrium.

**Decompression sickness (DCS)**: (also known as divers' disease, the bends or caisson disease) describes a condition arising from dissolved gases coming out of solution into bubbles inside the body on depressurisation. DCS most commonly refers to problems arising from underwater diving decompression but may be experienced in other depressurisation events such as emerging from a caisson, flying in an unpressurised aircraft at altitude, and extravehicular activity from spacecraft.

Since bubbles can form in or migrate to any part of the body, DCS can produce many symptoms, and its effects may vary from joint pain and rashes to paralysis and death. Individual susceptibility can vary from day to day, and different individuals under the same conditions may be affected differently or not at all. The classification of types of DCS by symptoms has evolved since its original description over a hundred years ago.

Risk of DCS caused by diving can be managed through proper decompression procedures. Its potential severity has driven much research to prevent it and divers almost universally use dive tables or dive computers to limit their exposure and to control their ascent speed. If DCS is suspected, it is treated by hyperbaric oxygen therapy in a recompression chamber.

**Decompression Illnesses (DCI)**: A catch-all term given to DCS and arterial gas embolism.

**Decompression stress**: sub-clinical symptoms such as fatigue and general malaise, caused by bubbles in the body post-dive. Also, the biochemical changes induced in the body by decompression not necessarily perceived as symptoms.

**Desaturation**: the process of becoming unsaturated

**Deterministic:** from determinism, the philosophical doctrine that every state of affairs, including every human event, act, and decision, is the inevitable consequence of previous states of affairs. In diving decompression, deterministic models define the outcome of a decompression as either "*bent*" or "*not bent*".

**Diuresis**: urine production by the kidneys

**Dive tender**: a surface member of a diving team who works closely with the diver on the bottom. At the start of a dive, the tender checks the diver's equipment and topside air supply for proper operation and dresses the diver. Once the diver is in the water, the tender constantly tends the lines to eliminate excess slack or tension. The tender exchanges line-pull signals with the diver, keeps the Diving Supervisor informed of the line-pull signals and amount of diving hose/tending line over the side and remains alert for any signs of an emergency.

**Doppler echocardiography**: (see also Echocardiography below), a procedure that uses ultrasound technology to examine the heart or blood vessels. An echocardiogram uses high-frequency sound waves to create an image of the heart while the use of Doppler technology allows determination of the speed and direction of blood flow by utilizing the Doppler effect.

**Echography:** refers to medical sonography. An echograph is more commonly called an ultrasound apparatus.

**Echocardiography**: a process that creates sonograms of the heart. Echocardiography uses standard two-dimensional, three-dimensional, and Doppler ultrasound to create images of the heart. Echocardiography has become routinely used in the diagnosis, management, and follow-up of patients with any suspected or known heart diseases. It is one of the most widely used diagnostic tests in cardiology. It can provide a wealth of helpful information, including the size and shape of the heart (internal chamber size quantification), pumping capacity, and the location and extent of any tissue damage. An echocardiogram can also give physicians other estimates of heart function, such as a calculation of the cardiac output, ejection fraction, and diastolic function, which is a term describing how well the heart relaxes.

Not only can an echocardiogram create ultrasound images of heart structures, but it can also produce an accurate assessment of the blood flowing through the heart by Doppler echocardiography, using pulsed- or continuous-wave Doppler ultrasound. This allows the assessment of both normal and abnormal blood flow through the heart. Colour Doppler and spectral Doppler are used to visualize any abnormal communications between the left and right sides of the heart, any leaking of blood through the valves (valvular regurgitation), and estimate how well the valves open (or do not open in the case of valvular stenosis).

**Echolocation**: the determination of the position of an object by measuring the time taken for an echo to return from it and its direction.

**Endothelium**: the inner lining of blood vessels, composed of a thin layer of endothelial cells. Endothelial cells in direct contact with blood are called vascular endothelial cells. Vascular endothelial cells line the entire circulatory system, from the heart to the smallest capillaries. Their functions include the maintenance of blood vessel tone.

**Endothelins**: peptides that constrict blood vessels and raise blood pressure.

**Flow-mediated dilation**: the flow-mediated dilation test is the most commonly used non-invasive assessment of vascular endothelial function in humans. The diameter of the brachial artery is measured by high-resolution ultrasound, once before placing a tourniquet on the upper or lower part of the arm, and then again after release of the tourniquet.

**Free phase gas**: bubbles.

**Heat shock proteins (HSP)**: a family of proteins that are produced by cells in response to exposure to stressful conditions.

**Hemoconcentration**: increased concentration of cells and solids in the blood usually resulting from loss of fluid to the tissues

**Hydrophobic**: Repelling water, tending not to combine with water or incapable of dissolving in water.

**Hyperbaric**: a pressure higher than normal atmospheric pressure.

**Hypogonadism**: diminished functional activity of the gonads, that is, the testes in males or the ovaries in females.

**Hypophyseal**: pertaining to the pituitary gland.

**Hyperoxia:** occurs when cells, tissues and organs are exposed to an excess supply of oxygen or a higher-than-normal partial pressure of oxygen.

**Hypertension**: also known as high blood pressure, is a medical condition in which the blood pressure in the arteries is persistently elevated.

**Hypovolemic shock**: an emergency condition in which severe blood or fluid loss makes the heart unable to pump enough blood to the body, causing many organs to stop working

**IDAN**: International Divers Alert Network

**Iontophoresis**, also known as Ionization, is a physical process in which ions flow diffusively in a medium driven by the use of an electric current.

**Ischemia**: a restriction in blood supply to tissues, causing a shortage of oxygen and glucose needed to keep the tissues alive.

**Kinetic**: relating to the motion of bodies and associated forces and energy

**kPa**: The Pascal (symbol: Pa) is a unit of pressure. It is defined as one newton per square metre. One kilopascal (kPa) is 1000 Pa and equals 100 Bar.

**Lung surfactant**: a surface-active lipoprotein complex formed by type II alveolar cells lining the lung sacs (alveoli). The proteins and lipids that make up the surfactant have both hydrophilic and hydrophobic regions.

**Marginal DCS events**: decompression sickness events characterised by vague symptoms, making the precise diagnosis of DCS difficult.

**mBar**: Millibar = 1/1000 of a bar. 1 mBar is equal to 100 Pascal or 1 hPa (hectopascal)

**Meyer-Overton Hypothesis**: the first hypothesis about nitrogen narcosis, stating that the penetration of lipid-soluble gases into the cell wall of neurons causes thickening of this cell wall, thus decreasing the speed of transmission of neuron electric signals.

**Microcirculation** is the circulation of the blood in the smallest blood vessels. The microcirculation is composed of terminal arterioles, capillaries and venules that drain capillary blood.

**Micronuclei**: the (presumed, as they have not yet been visualised directly) very small quantities of gas molecules that exist in a gaseous state somewhere in the blood vessels – probably in crevices in between the endothelial cells; these are presumed to accumulate more inert gas during decompression and grow into observable gas bubbles.

**micro-particles**: small membrane-bound vesicles circulating in the blood, derived from cells that are in contact with the bloodstream, such as platelets and endothelial cells. Because they retain the signature membrane protein composition of the parent cell, micro-particles carry useful information.

**Microspheres**: spherical micro-particles.

**M-value**: the "M" in M-value stands for Maximum. For a given ambient pressure, an M-value is defined as the maximum value of inert gas pressure that a hypothetical tissue compartment can tolerate without presenting overt symptoms of DCS.

**Neurological** DCS: another way of referring to Type II DCS (see below)

**Nitric oxide (NO):** one of several oxides of nitrogen and a colourless gas under standard conditions. In mammals including humans, nitric oxide is an important cellular signalling molecule involved in many physiological and pathological processes. It is a powerful vasodilator with a short half-life of a few seconds in the blood. As a consequence of its importance in neuroscience, physiology, and immunology, nitric oxide was proclaimed Molecule of the Year in 1992. Research into its function led to the 1998 Nobel Prize for discovering the role of nitric oxide as a cardiovascular signalling molecule.

**Normobaric**: a barometric pressure equivalent to the pressure at sea level.

**Normoxic**: having a normal oxygen concentration of 20-21% in the atmosphere. In trimix diving, normoxic refers to the use of a trimix gas that is still breathable at the surface, i.e. containing at least 18% of oxygen

**Nucleation**: the first step in the formation of either a new thermodynamic phase or a new structure, used in decompression research as one of the mechanisms of bubble formation. Heterogeneous nucleation occurs at nucleation sites on surfaces in the system. Homogeneous nucleation occurs away from a surface.

**Oesophagus**: the food pipe or gullet.

**Oscillation**: the repetitive variation of some measure about a central value or between two or more different states. Familiar examples of oscillation include a swinging pendulum, alternating current power and the human heart.

**Oxidative stress:** an imbalance between the manifestation of reactive oxygen species and a biological system's ability to readily detoxify them or repair the resulting damage.

**Parasternal**: beside the sternum.

**PPO2**: partial pressure of oxygen

**Pathology:** the study of disease in general. Pathology can also refer to the predicted or actual progression of a particular disease, as in the statement *"The many different forms of cancer have diverse pathologies*". A pathological condition is one caused by disease, rather than occurring physiologically.

**Pathophysiology**: the convergence of pathology with physiology. Pathophysiology can also mean the functional changes associated with or resulting from disease or injury. Another definition is the functional changes that accompany a particular disease.

**Perfusion**: the passage of fluid through the circulatory system or lymphatic system to an organ or a tissue, usually referring to the delivery of blood to a capillary bed in tissue.

**Permeability**: the rate of flow of a liquid or gas through a porous material.

**Peroxynitrite**: an oxidant and nitrating agent. Because of its oxidizing properties, peroxynitrite can damage a wide array of molecules in cells, including DNA and proteins. Formation of peroxynitrite *in vivo* has been ascribed to the reaction of the free radical superoxide with the free radical nitric oxide. The resultant pairing of these two free radicals results in peroxynitrite, a molecule that, while itself not a free radical, is nevertheless a powerful oxidant.

**PFO**: there is a congenital heart condition known as an atrial septal defect in which blood can in some circumstances flow between the right and left atria (upper chambers) of the heart. Normally, the atria are separated by a dividing wall, the interatrial septum. If this septum is defective or absent, then oxygen-rich blood can flow directly from the left side of the heart to mix with the oxygen-poor blood in the right side of the heart, an atrial septal defect, or vice versa, a PFO. A "shunt" is the word given to the presence of a net flow of blood through the defect, either from left to right or right to left. During the development of the foetus, the interatrial septum develops to separate the left and right atria. However, a hole in the septum called the foramen ovale allows blood from the right atrium to enter the left atrium during foetal development. This opening allows blood to bypass the non-functional foetal lungs while the foetus obtains its oxygen from the placenta. A layer of tissue called the septum primum acts as a valve over the foramen ovale during foetal development.

After birth, the pressure in the right side of the heart drops as the lungs open and begin working, causing the foramen ovale to close entirely. In about 25% of adults, the foramen ovale does not entirely seal. In these cases, any elevation of the pressure in the pulmonary circulatory system can cause the foramen ovale to remain open. This is known as a patent foramen ovale (PFO), which is not necessarily a type of atrial septal defect. However, it is closely associated.

**Phospholipids**: a class of lipids that are a major component of all cell membranes.

**Physiology**: the scientific study of normal mechanisms, and their interactions, which operate within a living system. A sub-discipline of biology, its focus is on how organisms, organ systems, organs, cells and biomolecules carry out the chemical or physical functions that exist in a living system.

**Pneumogauge**: a precision pressure gauge used for diver depth monitoring or for measuring the pressure within a hyperbaric chamber

**PO2**: the pressure of oxygen, often used interchangeably with PPO2.

**Poisson distribution**: a discrete probability distribution that expresses the probability of a given number of events occurring in a fixed interval of time and/or space if these events occur with a known average rate and independently of the time since the last event. The Poisson distribution can also be used for the number of events in other specified intervals such as distance, area or volume.

For instance, an individual keeping track of the amount of mail they receive each day may notice that they receive an average of 4 letters per day. If receiving any particular piece of mail doesn't affect the arrival times of future pieces of mail, i.e., if pieces of mail from a wide range of sources arrive independently of one another, then a reasonable assumption is that the number of pieces of mail received per day obeys a Poisson distribution.

Another example that may follow a Poisson distribution is the number of phone calls received by a call centre per hour.

**Probabilistic**: based on, or affected by probability, randomness, or chance.

**Prostacyclin**: **a** member of the eicosanoid family of lipid molecules. It inhibits platelet activation and is also an effective vasodilator.

**PubMed** is a free search engine accessing primarily the MEDLINE database of references and abstracts on life sciences and biomedical topics.

**Pyle stops**: short decompression stops at depths well below the first decompression stop mandated by a conventional decompression algorithm. They were named after Dr Richard Pyle, an American ichthyologist from Hawaii, who found that they prevented post-dive fatigue symptoms after deep dives to collect fish specimens. These stops were developed by Pyle based on personal experience and have had a significant influence on decompression theory and practice in the following since the mid-1990s.

**Redundant**: adjective applied in technical diving parlance to excess or duplicate equipment that can be deployed by a diver in the event of malfunction of the diver's primary equipment.

**Rheology**: the study of the flow of matter, primarily in a liquid state.

**Saturation**: the state of being saturated, of maximum impregnation. In diving, also used to refer to the progressive increase of inert gas pressures in the tissues when a diver is breathing a gas mix with a higher inert gas pressure.

**Saturation vapour pressure**: The pressure exhibited by vapour present above a liquid surface is known as vapour pressure. As the temperature of a liquid increases, the kinetic energy of its molecules also increases. As the kinetic energy of the molecules increases, the number of molecules transitioning into a vapour also increases, thereby increasing the vapour pressure.

The vapour pressure of any substance increases non-linearly with temperature. The normal boiling point of a liquid is the temperature at which the vapour pressure equals the ambient atmospheric pressure. With any incremental increase in that temperature, the vapour pressure becomes sufficient to overcome atmospheric pressure and lift the liquid to form vapour bubbles inside the bulk of the substance.

Bubble formation deeper in the liquid requires higher pressure, and therefore higher temperature, because the fluid pressure increases above the atmospheric pressure as the depth increases. The surface tension of the bubble wall leads to an overpressure in very small, initial bubbles.

**Sepsis**: is a life-threatening condition that arises when the body's response to infection causes injury to its own tissues and organs.

**Serum**: the component of the blood that is neither a blood cell nor a clotting factor. It is the blood plasma not including the fibrinogens. Serum includes all proteins not used in blood clotting and all the electrolytes, antibodies, antigens and hormones.

**Shunt**: a hole or a small passage which moves, or allows movement of, fluid from one part of the body to another. Cardiac shunts may be described as right-to-left, left-to-right or bidirectional.

**Silent bubbles**: micro-bubbles that form in the bloodstream of all scuba divers, but which do not produce any detectable symptoms.

**Striatum**: one of the nuclei in the subcortical basal ganglia of the forebrain. Functionally, the striatum coordinates multiple aspects of cognition, including motor- and action-planning, decision-making, motivation, reinforcement, and reward perception.

**Sub-acute**: somewhat acute; between acute and chronic. Denoting the course of a disease of moderate duration or severity.

**Subclavian vein**: The **subclavian vein** is a paired large vein, one on either side of the body. Their diameter is approximately that of the smallest finger.

**Sub-clinical**: describing a disease or injury, without signs and symptoms that are detectable by physical examination or laboratory test.

**Superoxide anion**: an oxygen free radical.

**Supersaturation**: a state of a solution that contains more of the dissolved material than could be dissolved under normal circumstances.

**Tetrahydrobiopterin**: a naturally occurring essential cofactor of the three aromatic amino acid hydroxylase enzymes.

**Thalamocortical pathway**: the connection between the thalamus and the cerebral cortex.

**Thermodynamics**: thermodynamics is a branch of physics concerned with heat and temperature and their relation to energy and work.

**Tissue**: an ensemble of similar cells from the same origin that together carry out a specific function. Organs are formed by the functional grouping together of multiple tissues.

**Transducer**: a device that converts energy from one form to another. Usually, a transducer converts a signal in one form of energy to a signal in another.

**Transoesophageal**: through or across the oesophagus.

**Transthoracic**: through the thoracic cavity or across the chest wall.

**Tribonucleation**: a mechanism that creates small gas bubbles by the action of making and breaking contact between solid surfaces immersed in a liquid containing dissolved gas. These small bubbles may then act as nuclei for the growth of bubbles when the pressure is reduced. As the formation of the nuclei occurs quite easily, the effect may occur in a human body engaged in light exercise, yet produce no symptoms. However, tribonucleation may be a source of growing bubbles affecting scuba divers when ascending to the surface and is a potential cause of decompression sickness.

**Type I DCS / Type II DCS**: In 1960, Golding et al. introduced a simple DCS classification using the term "Type I (simple)" for symptoms involving only the skin, musculoskeletal system or lymphatic system, and "Type II (serious)" for symptoms where other organs, such as the central nervous system, were involved. Type II DCS usually had worse outcomes. This classification, with minor modifications, is still used today, but is now not so useful from a diagnosis point of view, since it is now known that neurological symptoms can develop after the initial presentation and both Type I and Type II require the same initial management.

**Valsalva manoeuvre**: this is performed by moderately forceful attempted exhalation against a closed airway, usually done by closing one's mouth, then pinching one's nose shut while pressing out as if blowing up a balloon. It is used to "clear" the ears and sinuses (that is, to equalize pressure between them) when ambient pressure changes, as in diving, hyperbaric oxygen therapy, or air travel. The technique is named after Antonio Maria Valsalva, a seventeenth-century physician and anatomist from Bologna.

**Vasoconstriction**: the narrowing of the blood vessels resulting from contraction of the muscular wall of the vessels, in particular the large arteries and small arterioles. The process is the opposite of vasodilation, the widening of blood vessels, (see below).

**Vasodilation**: the widening of blood vessels, resulting from the relaxation of smooth muscle cells within the vessel walls, in particular in the large veins, large arteries, and smaller arterioles. The process is the opposite of vasoconstriction, which is the narrowing of blood vessels, (see above).

**Vena cava**: Either of two large veins that drain blood from the upper body and from the lower body and empty into the right atrium of the heart. The inferior vena cava is the venous trunk for the lower extremities. The superior vena cava is the venous trunk draining blood from the head, neck, upper extremities, and chest.

**Venous system-arterial system**: Although the cardiovascular system is referred to as one unit, it is actually two separate systems which work independently. Through the arterial supply, oxygenated blood is distributed from the left heart and aorta, eventually to every cell in the body. The arteries divide into smaller arteries, then into arterioles, which in turn divide into capillaries. Oxygen exchange takes place in the capillaries; vessels whose walls are only one cell thick. In the venous system, deoxygenated blood drains from the capillaries, which conjoin into venules, small veins, veins, and the major draining vessels, the superior and inferior venae cavae (see above). This blood then enters the right heart and travels to the lungs to re-oxygenate and start the cycle again. Note that, in general, any blood vessel that leads blood AWAY from the heart is called an "artery." Thus, the pulmonary artery brings deoxygenated blood from the right ventricle to the lungs. Any vessel that leads blood TOWARDS the heart is called a vein. Thus, the pulmonary veins bring oxygenated blood from the lungs to the left atrium.

# ACRONYMS

AGE: Arterial Gas Embolism

ATA: Atmospheres Absolute

ATM: Atmosphere

BCD: Buoyancy Control Device

BH4: Tetrahydrobiopterin

CFFF: Critical Flicker Fusion Frequency

CCR: Closed-Circuit Rebreather

DAN: Divers Alert Network

DCI: Decompression Illnesses

DCIEM: Defence and Civil Institute of Environmental Medicine

DCS: Decompression Sickness

DDC: Deck Decompression Chamber

DNA: Deoxyribonucleic Acid

DSL: Dan Europe Diving Safety Laboratory

DSV: Diving Support Vessel

EB: Eftedal-Brubakk scale

EDCF: Endothelium-Dependent Constricting Factor

EDTC: European Diving Technology Committee

EEG: Electro-encephalogram

EDRF: Endothelium-Dependent Relaxing Factor

FMD: Flow Mediated Dilation

GF's: Gradient Factors

HPNS: High-Pressure Nervous Syndrome

HSE: Health & Safety Executive

IDANRCAPP: International Divers Alert Network Recompression Chamber Assistance & Partnership Programme

IFP: Institut Français du Pétrole

IPAVA: Intra Pulmonary Arterio-Venous Anastomoses

KISS: Kisman Integrated Severity Score

KM: Kisman-Masurel scale

kPa: kilo-Pascal

NPD: Norwegian Petroleum Directorate

NEDU: The US Navy Experimental Diving Unit

NIRS: Near Infrared Spectroscopy

NO: Nitric Oxide

PEBL: Psychology Experiment Building Language

PFO: Patent Foramen Ovale

PFSI: Pre-Flight Surface Interval

PPO2 / PO2: (Partial) Pressure of Oxygen

PORH: Post-occlusive Reactive Hyperaemia

PPE: Personal Protective Equipment

PTC: Personnel Transfer Capsule

RCAPP: Recompression Chamber Assistance & Partnership Program

RGBM: Reduced Gradient Bubble Model

RNPL: Royal Naval Physiological Laboratory

SCUBA: (Yes, it's an acronym) Self-Contained Underwater Breathing Apparatus

SPG: Submersible Pressure Gauge

TTE: Transthoracic Echocardiography

TUP: Transfer Under Pressure

VGE: Vascular Gas Emboli

VPM: Varying Permeability Model

VSM: Vascular Smooth Muscle

ZHL: Zurich (ZH) Limits (Prof. Bühlmann lived in Zurich)

## AUTHOR / EDITOR: SCUBA PHYSIOLOGICAL

Simon Pridmore writes scuba diving books, travel books and, as you might expect, scuba diving travel books. Over the years he has written hundreds of magazine articles on diver training, dive safety and dive destinations and is a frequent speaker at conferences all over the world. Simon and his wife Sofie currently live in Taiwan but travel widely, always looking for a cure for their itchy feet.

Find out more on www.simonpridmore.com

# ALSO BY SIMON PRIDMORE

## SCUBA DIVING BOOKS

- Scuba Fundamental: Start Diving the Right Way
- Scuba Confidential: An Insider's Guide to Becoming a Better Diver
- Scuba Exceptional: Become the Best Diver You Can Be
- Scuba Professional: Insights into Sport Diver Training & Operations
- Technically Speaking - Talks on Technical Diving Volume One: Genesis and Exodus

## TRAVEL BOOKS

- Under the Flight Path: 15,000 kms Overland Across Russia, Mongolia & China
- Dive into Taiwan

## BIOGRAPHY

- The Diver Who Fell from the Sky

## FICTION

- May the People Know I'm Here?

## BY SIMON PRIDMORE WITH TIM ROCK

- Diving & Snorkeling Guide to Bali

- Diving & Snorkeling Guide to Raja Ampat & Northeast Indonesia
- The 50 Best Dives in Indonesia – The Ultimate Guide to the Essential Sites

**BY SIMON PRIDMORE WITH DAVID STRIKE**

- Dining with Divers: Tales from the Kitchen Table
- Dining with Divers: A Taste for Adventure

# THE ORIGINAL AUTHORS OF THE SCIENCE OF DIVING

**Costantino BALESTRA:** MSc, PhD; Full-time Professor and Head of the Environmental and Occupational Physiology (Integrative) Lab. at the Haute Ecole Paul Henri Spaak, BELGIUM; Vice-President DAN Europe Research & Education, ITALY; Area Director DAN Europe Benelux & France, President of the European Underwater & Baromedical Society, Motor Sciences Dept. Université Libre de Bruxelles, Belgium

**Jean-Eric BLATTEAU:** MD, PhD, Specialist in Diving and Hyperbaric medicine, President of the French Society of Subaquatic and Hyperbaric Medicine, Research Director, Head of Subaquatic Hyperbaric Operational Research Team from French Biomedical research Institute, IRBA/ ERRSO, Toulon, FRANCE

**Alain BOUSSUGES:** MD, PhD; Cardiologist and Research Director at French Armed Biomedical Research Institute (IRBA), Brétigny sur Orge, FRANCE; and UMR-MD2, Aix-Marseille University, Marseille, FRANCE

**Francois BURMAN:** MS, Pr. Eng; CEO at DAN Southern Africa, Pretoria, SOUTH AFRICA

**Peter BUZZACOTT:** MPH, PhD; PHYPODE ER (Experienced Researcher) at Université de Bretagne Occidentale, Optimisation des Régulations Physiologiques (ORPhy), UFR Sciences et Techniques, Brest, FRANCE; Adjunct lecturer at

School of Sports Science, Exercise and Health, The University of Western Australia, Crawley, WA, AUSTRALIA

**Danilo CIALONI**: DMD; PHYPODE ESR (Early Stage Researcher) and European Research Area Supervisor DAN Europe Foundation, Roseto degli Abruzzi, ITALY

**Zeljko DUJIC:** MD, PhD; Full-time Professor and Head of Department of Integrative Physiology; School of Medicine, University of Split, Split, CROATIA

**Robert J. ECKERSLEY:** PhD; Senior Lecturer in Biomedical Engineering in the Biomedical Engineering Department, Division of Imaging Sciences, King's College London, London, UNITED KINGDOM

**Murat S. EGI**: MSc, PhD; Associate Professor at Galatasaray University Computer Engineering Department, Istanbul, TURKEY; National Manager DAN Europe Türkiye, DAN Europe Foundation, Roseto degli Abruzzi, ITALY

**Emmanuel GEMPP**: MD; Senior Diving Medical Officer; Department of Diving and Hyperbaric Medicine, Sainte Anne Military Hospital, Toulon, FRANCE

**Peter GERMONPRE:** MD; Medical Director of the Centre for Hyperbaric Oxygen Therapy of the Military Hospital, Brussels, BELGIUM; Medical Director of Divers Alert Network Europe (Benelux & French Language Areas); Senior Research Associate, DAN Europe Research, Roseto degli Abruzzi, ITALY.

**Francois GUERRERO**: MSc, PhD. Full-time Professor at Université de Bretagne Occidentale, EA4324 Optimisation des Régulations Physiologiques (ORPhy), UFR Sport et Education Physique, Brest, FRANCE

**Walter HEMELRYCK**: MSc, Osteopath DO; PHYPODE ESR (Early Stage Researcher) at the Centre for Hyperbaric Oxygen Therapy, Military Hospital Brussels, and the Environmental & Occupational Physiology Laboratory of the Haute Ecole Paul Henri Spaak, Brussels, BELGIUM

**Jean-Pierre IMBERT:** MSc, Diving consultant, Divetech EURL, Biot, FRANCE

**Thodoris D. KARAPANTSIOS**: MSc, PhD; Full-time Professor at the Faculty of Chemistry, Aristotle University of Thessaloniki, Thessaloniki, GREECE

**Jacek KOT:** MD, PhD, Assistant Professor at the Medical University of Gdansk, National Centre for Hyperbaric Medicine in Gdynia, POLAND

**Pierre LAFÈRE:** MD, PhD; Department of Anaesthesiology and Hyperbaric Medicine, Hôpital de la Cavale Blanche, Brest, FRANCE

**Kate LAMBRECHTS:** MSc, PhD; PHYPODE ESR (Early Stage Researcher) at Université de Bretagne Occidentale, Optimisation des Régulations Physiologiques (ORPhy), UFR Sciences et Techniques, Brest, FRANCE

**Cecile LAVOUTE:** MSc, PhD; Senior Hospital Research Scientist at Department of Cardiology B, Hôpital de la Timone, Marseille, FRANCE

**Dennis MADDEN:** MSc; PHYPODE ESR (Early Stage Researcher) at School of Medicine, University of Split, CROATIA

**Alessandro MARRONI:** MD, PhD; President and CEO of DAN Europe Foundation, Roseto degli Abruzzi, ITALY; Chairman, International DAN; Vice President European Committee for Hyperbaric Medicine; Secretary General,

European College of Baromedicine; Professor (vis) of Baromedicine, International School of Baromedicine, University of Belgrade Medical School, SERBIA.

**Aleksandra MAZUR:** MSc, PhD; PHYPODE ESR (Early Stage Researcher) at Université de Bretagne Occidentale, Optimisation des Régulations Physiologiques (ORPhy), UFR Sciences et Techniques, Brest, FRANCE

**Tamer OZYIGIT:** MSc, PhD; Galatasaray University, Computer Engineering Department, Istanbul, TURKEY

**Virginie PAPADOPOULOU:** MSc; PHYPODE ESR (Early Stage Researcher) at the Biophysiology and Environmental Physiology Lab of the Haute Ecole Paul Henri Spaak (University of Brussels), BELGIUM; PhD Candidate at the Bioengineering Department of Imperial College London, London, UNITED KINGDOM

**Massimo PIERI:** European Research Area Supervisor, Data Collection Coordinator, DAN Europe Foundation, Roseto degli Abruzzi, ITALY

**Georgi POPOV:** MSc; PHYPODE ESR (Early Stage Researcher) at MARES Spa, Rapallo, ITALY

**Miroslav ROZLOZNIK**: MSc, PhD; PHYPODE ER (Experienced Researcher) at Environmental & Occupational Physiology Laboratory of the Haute Ecole Paul Henri Spaak, Brussels, BELGIUM

**Ahmed SAKR:** MD; Assistant Director of the Hyperbaric Medical Centre, Sharm el Sheikh, EGYPT

**Adel TAHER:** MD; National Director of DAN Egypt, Director of the Hyperbaric Medical Centre, Sharm el Sheikh, EGYPT

**Meng-Xing TANG:** PhD; Senior Lecturer in the Department of Bioengineering, Imperial College London, London, UNITED KINGDOM

**Guy THOMAS:** DMT; Executive Vice President Mission and Operations at DAN Europe Foundation, Roseto degli Abruzzi, ITALY

**Frauke TILLMANS:** MSc; PHYPODE ESR (Early Stage Researcher) at Environmental & Occupational Physiology Laboratory of the Haute Ecole Paul Henri Spaak, Brussels, BELGIUM

**Yurii TKACHENKO:** MD; PHYPODE ESR (Early Stage Researcher) at Medical University of Gdansk, National Centre for Hyperbaric Medicine in Gdynia, POLAND

**Qiong WANG:** MSc, PhD; PHYPODE ESR (Early Stage Researcher) at Université de Bretagne Occidentale, Optimisation des Régulations Physiologiques (ORPhy), UFR Sciences et Techniques, Brest, FRANCE.

# REFERENCES & FURTHER READING

## Chapter 2


- *Papadopoulou V, Eckersley RJ, Balestra C, Karapantsios TD, Tang MX. A critical review of physiological bubble formation in hyperbaric decompression. Adv Colloid Interface Sci. 2013;191-192:22-30.*
- *Papadopoulou V, Tang MX, Balestra C, Eckersley RJ, Karapantsios TD. Circulatory bubble dynamics: from physical to biological aspects. Adv Colloid Interface Sci. 2014;206:239-49.*
- *Hemelryck W, Germonpré P, Papadopoulou V, Rozloznik M, Balestra C. Long term effects of recreational SCUBA diving on higher cognitive function. Scand J Med Sci Spor. 2013*
- *Madden D, Thom SR, Yang M, Bhopale VM, Ljubkovic M, Dujic Z. High intensity cycling before SCUBA diving reduces post-decompression microparticle production and neutrophil activation. Eur J Appl Physiol. 2014*
- *Culic VC, Van Craenenbroeck E, Muzinic NR, Ljubkovic M, Marinovic J, Conraads V, et al. Effects of scuba diving*

*on vascular repair mechanisms. Undersea Hyperb Med. 2014;41:97-104.*

- *Zanchi J, Ljubkovic M, Denoble PJ, Dujic Z, Ranapurwala S, Pollock NW. Influence of repeated daily diving on decompression stress. Int J Sports Med. 2014;35:465-8.*

## Chapter 3

- *Blogg SL., Lang MA., Møllerløkken A. (Eds.) Proceedings of Validation of Dive Computers Workshop. Gdansk, Poland, 2011.*
- *Denoble P. The validation of dive computer decompression safety. Alert Diver Magazine (Summer 2010), Divers Alert Network, Durham, NC.*
- *Egi SM, Gurmen NM. Computation of decompression tables using continuous compartment half-lives. Undersea Hyperb Med 2000;27:143-153.*
- *Gempp E, Blatteau JE, Pontier JM, Balestra C and Louge P. Preventive effect of pre-dive hydration on bubble formation in divers. Br J Sports Med 2009; 43:224-228.*
- *Lang MA, Brubakk AO. (Eds.) The Future of Diving: 100 Years of Haldane and Beyond. Trondheim, Norway, 2009. Smithsonian Scholarly Press, Washington, DC.*
- *Lang MA, Angelini SA. The Future of Dive Computers. In: Lang MA, Brubakk AO. (Eds). The Future of Diving: 100 Years of Haldane and Beyond. Smithsonian Scholarly Press, Washington, DC. pp. 91-100.*

## Chapter 4

- *Boycott AE, Damant GC, Haldane JS. The prevention of compressed-air illness. J Hyg (Lond) 1908;8(3):342-443.*

- *Brubakk AO, Neuman TS (Eds.) Bennett and Elliott's Physiology and Medicine of Diving. 5th Edition. Saunders, Philadelphia, PA, 2003.*
- *Doolette DJ. Development and testing of deterministic and probabilistic decompression models. SPUMS J 2005;35:28-31.*
- *Doolette DJ, Mitchell SJ. Recreational technical diving - Part 2: Decompression from deep technical dives. Diving Hyperb Med 2013;43:96-104.*
- *Huggins KE. Dynamics of decompression workshop. University of Michigan, 1992.*
- *Lang MA, Brubakk AO. (Eds): The Future of Diving: 100 Years of Haldane and Beyond. Smithsonian Scholarly Press, Washington, DC. 2009*
- *Le Messurier DH, Hills BA. Decompression Sickness. A thermodynamic approach arising from a study on Torres Strait diving techniques. H Valdradets Skrifter 1965;48:54-84.*
- *US Navy Diving Manual (6th Revised Edition). Naval Sea Systems Command. Aquapress, Southend-on-Sea, UK, 2010.*
- *Powell M. Deco for divers: a diver's guide to decompression theory and physiology. Aquapress, Southend-on-Sea; UK, 2008.*
- *Papadopoulou V, Eckersley RJ, Balestra C, Karapantsios TD, Tang M-X. A critical review of physiological bubble formation in hyperbaric decompression. Adv Colloid Interface Sci 2013;191-192:22-30*
- *Papadopoulou V, Tang M-X, Balestra C, Eckersley RJ, Karapantsios TD. Circulatory bubble dynamics: from physical to biological aspects. Adv Colloid Interface Sci. 2014;206C:239-249.*

- *Wienke BR. Basic Decompression. Theory and Application, 3rd Edition. Best Publishing, Flagstaff, AZ, 2008.*
- *Yount DE. Gelatin, bubbles, and the bends. In: Hans-Jurgen K, Harper Jr, DE (Eds.). Proceedings of the American Academy of Underwater Sciences Eleventh Annual Scientific Diving Symposium. University of Hawaii, Honolulu, Hawaii, 1991: pp 127-142.*


## Chapter 5


- *Cheney FW, Pavlin J, Ferens J, Allen D. Effect of pulmonary microembolism on arteriovenous shunt flow. J Thorac Cardiovasc Surg 1978;76:473-478.*
- *Eldridge MW, Dempsey JA, Haverkamp HC, Lovering AT, Hokanson JS. Exercise-induced intrapulmonary arteriovenous shunting in healthy humans. J Appl Physiol 2004;97:797-805.*
- *Ljubkovic M, Dujic Z, Mollerlokken A, Bakovic D, Obad A, Breskovic T, Brubakk AO. Venous and arterial bubbles at rest after no-decompression air dives. Med Sci Sports Exerc 2011; 43:990-995.*
- *Ljubkovic M, Zanchi J, Breskovic T, Marinovic J, Lojpur M, Dujic Z. Determinants of arterial gas embolism after SCUBA diving. J Appl Physiol 2012;112:91-95.*
- *Lovering AT, Stickland MK, Kelso AJ, Eldridge MW. Direct demonstration of 25- and 50-micrometer arteriovenous pathways in healthy human and baboon lungs. Am J Physiol Heart Circ Physiol 2007;292:H1777-1781.*
- *Meltzer RS, Sartorius OE, Lancee CT, Serruys PW, Verdouw PD, Essed CE, Roelandt J. Transmission of ultrasonic contrast through the lungs. Ultrasound Med Biol 1981;7:377-384.*

- *Thom SR, Milovanova TN, Bogush M, Yang M, Bhopale VM, Pollock NW, Ljubkovic M, Denoble PJ, Madden D, Lozo M, Dujic Z. Bubbles, micro-particles and neutrophil activation: changes with exercise level and breathing gas during open-water scuba diving. J Appl Physiol 2013; 114(10):1396-405.*
- *Tobin CE, Zariquiey MO. Arteriovenous shunts in the human lung. Proc Soc Exp Biol Med 1950; 75:827-829.*
- *Butler BD, Hills BA. The lung as a filter for microbubbles. J Appl Physiol 1979; 47(3):537-43.*
- *Balestra C, Germonpré P, Marroni A, Cronjé FJ. PFO and the diver. Best Publishing, Flagstaff, AZ, 2007.*
- *Germonpré P. Patent Foramen Ovale and Diving. Cardiol Clin 2005;23:97–104.*


## Chapter 6


- *Brubakk AO, Duplancic D, Valic Z, Palada I, Obad A, Bakovic D, Wisloff U, Dujic Z. A single air dive reduces arterial endothelial function in man. J Physiol 2005; 566:901-906.*
- *Brunner FP, Frick PG, Buhlmann AA. Post-Decompression Shock Due to Extravasation of Plasma. Lancet 1964; 1:1071-1073.*
- *Dujic Z, Duplancic D, Marinovic-Terzic I, Bakovic D, Ivancev V, Valic Z, Eterovic D, Petri NM, Wisloff U, Brubakk AO. Aerobic exercise before diving reduces venous gas bubble formation in humans. J Physiol 2004; 555:637-642.*
- *Dujic Z, Palada I, Valic Z, Duplancic D, Obad A, Wisloff U, Brubakk AO. Exogenous nitric oxide and bubble formation in divers. Med Sci Sports Exerc 2006; 38:1432-1435.*

- *Lambrechts K, Pontier M, Balestra C, Mazur A, Wang Q, Buzzacott P, Theron M, Mansourati J, Guerrero F. Effect of a single, open-sea, air scuba dive on human micro- and macrovascular function. Eur J Appl Physiol 2013; 113(10): 2637-45.*
- *Madden LA, Laden G. Gas bubbles may not be the underlying cause of decompression illness - the at-depth endothelial dysfunction hypothesis. Med Hypoth 2009; 72:389-392.*
- *Obad A, Marinovic J, Ljubkovic M, Breskovic T, Modun D, Boban M, Dujic Z. Successive deep dives impair endothelial function and enhance oxidative stress in man. Clin Physiol Funct Imaging 2010; 30:432-438.*
- *Obad A, Palada I, Valic Z, Ivancev V, Bakovic D, Wisloff U, Brubakk AO, Dujic Z. The effects of acute oral antioxidants on diving-induced alterations in human cardiovascular function. J Physiol 2007; 578:859-870.*
- *Obad A, Valic Z, Palada I, Brubakk AO, Modun D, Dujic Z. Antioxidant pretreatment and reduced arterial endothelial dysfunction after diving. Aviat Space Environm Med 2007; 78:1114-1120.*
- *Pontier JM, Guerrero F, Castagna O. Bubble formation and endothelial function before and after 3 months of dive training. Aviat Space Environm Med 2009; 80:15-19.*
- *Theunissen S, Guerrero F, Sponsiello N, Cialoni D, Pieri M, Germonpré P, Obeid G, Tillmans F, Papadopoulou V, Hemelryck W, Marroni A, De Bels D, Balestra C. Nitric oxide-related endothelial changes in breath-hold and scuba divers. Undersea Hyperb Med 2013; 40:135-144.*
- *Thom SR, Yang M, Bhopale VM, Huang S, Milovanova TN. micro-particles initiate decompression-induced neutrophil activation and subsequent vascular injuries. J Appl Physiol 2011; 110:340-351.*

## Chapter 7


- *Gillis MF, Petersen P, Karangianes MT. In vivo detection of circulating gas emboli with decompression sickness using the Doppler flow-meter. Nature 1968; 217: 965-967.*
- *Spencer MP. Decompression limits for compressed air determined by ultrasonically detected blood bubbles. J Appl Physiol 1976; 40(2):229-235.*
- *Beck TW, Daniel S, Paton WDM, Smith EB. Detection of bubbles in decompression sickness. Nature 1978; 276: 173-174.*
- *Boussuges A, Carturan D, Ambrosi P, Habib G, Sainty JM, Luccioni R. Decompression induced venous gas emboli in sport diving: detection with 2D echocardiography and pulsed Doppler. Int J Sports Med 1998; 19(1):7-11.*
- *Buckey JC, Knaus DA, Alvarenga DL, Kenton MA, Magari PJ. Dual-frequency ultrasound for detecting and sizing bubbles. Acta Astronautica 2005; 56:1041-47.*
- *Swan G, Bollinger BD, Donoghue TG, Wilbur JC, Phillips SD, Alvarenga DL, Knaus DA, Magari PJ, Buckey JC. Microbubble detection following hyperbaric chamber dives using Dual–Frequency Ultrasound. J Appl Physiol 2011; 111(5):1323-1328.*
- *Blogg SL, Gennser M. The need for optimisation of post-dive ultrasound monitoring to properly evaluate the evolution of venous gas emboli. Diving Hyperb Med 2011; 41(3):139-146*
- *Brubakk AO, Neuman TS. (Eds.) Bennett and Elliott's Physiology and Medicine of Diving. 5th Edition. Saunders, Philadelphia, PA, 2003.*
- *Parlak IB, Egi SM, Ademoglu A, Germonpré P, Esen OB, Marroni A, Balestra C. Bubble stream reveals functionality of the right-to-left shunt: Detection of a*

*potential source for air embolism. Ultrasound Med Biol 2014; 40(2):330-340.*

- *Eftedal OS. Ultrasonic detection of decompression induced vascular microbubbles. Doctoral Thesis, NTNU, Norway, 2007.*
- *Germonpré P, Papadopoulou V, Hemelryck W, Obeid G, Eckersley RJ, Tang M-X, Balestra C. The use of portable 2D echocardiography and "frame-based" bubble counting as a tool to evaluate diving decompression stress. Diving Hyperb Med 2014; 44:5-13.*
- *Papadopoulou V, Hui J, Balestra C, Hemelryck W, Germonpré P, Eckersley R, Tang M-X. Automated Counting of Venous Gas Emboli in Post-SCUBA Dive Echocardiography. Presented at the IEEE Ultrasonics, Ferroelectrics and Frequency Control Joint Symposium. Prague, Czech Republic. 22-25 July 2013.*

## Chapter 8

- *Blatteau JE, Gempp E, Balestra C, Mets T, Germonpré P. Pre-dive sauna and venous gas bubbles upon decompression from 400 kPa. Aviat Space Environm Med 2008; 79:1100-1105.*
- *Castagna O, Gempp E, Blatteau JE. Pre-dive normobaric oxygen reduces bubble formation in SCUBA divers. Eur J Appl Physiol 2009; 106(2):167-172.*
- *Castagna O, Brisswalter J, Vallee N, Blatteau JE. Endurance exercise immediately before sea diving reduces bubble formation in SCUBA divers. Eur J Appl Physiol 2011; 111(6):1047-54.*
- *Gempp E, Blatteau JE, Pontier JM, Balestra C, Louge P. Preventive effect of pre-dive hydration on bubble formation in divers. Br J Sports Med 2009; 43:224-228.*

- *Gempp E, Blatteau JE. Preconditioning methods and mechanisms for preventing the risk of decompression sickness in SCUBA divers: a review. Res Sports Med 2010; 18(3):205-18.*
- *Germonpré P, Pontier JM, Gempp E, Blatteau JE, Deneweth S, Lafère P, Marroni A, Balestra C. Pre-dive vibration effect on bubble formation after a 30-m dive requiring a decompression stop. Aviat Space Environm Med 2009; 80(12):1044-1048.*
- *Theunissen S, Schumacker J, Guerrero F, Tillmans F, Boutros A, Lambrechts K, Mazur A, Pieri M, Germonpré P, Balestra C. Dark chocolate reduces endothelial dysfunction after successive breath-hold dives in cool water. Our J App Physiol 2013; 113(12):2967-2975.*
- *Theunissen S, Guerrero F, Sponsiello N, Cialoni D, Pieri M, Germonpré P, Obeid G, Tillmans F, Papadopoulou V, Hemelryck W, Marroni A, De Bels D, Balestra C. Nitric oxide-related endothelial changes in breath-hold and SCUBA divers. Undersea Hyperb Med 2013; 40:135-144.*
- *Obad A, Palada I, Valic Z, Ivancev V, Bakovic D, Wisloff U, Brubakk AO, Dujic Z. The effects of acute oral antioxidants on diving-induced alterations in human cardiovascular function. J Physiol 2007; 578(3):859-870.*


**Chapter 9**


- *Benton MJ, Glover MA. Dive Medicine. Travel Med Infect Dis 2006; 4:238-254.*
- *Buch AD, Moalem HE, Dovenbarger JA, Uguccioni DM, Moon RE. Cigarette smoking and decompression illness severity: a retrospective study in recreational divers. Aviat Space Environ Med 2003; 74:1271-1278.*

- *Dilts D, Khamalah J, Plotkin A. Using cluster analysis for medical resource decision making. Med Decis Making 1995; 15:333-347.*
- *Golding FC, Griffiths P, Hempleman HV, Paton WDM, Walder DN. Decompression sickness during construction of the Dartford Tunnel. Brit J Indust Med 1960; 17:167-180.*
- *Hand D, Mannila H, Smyth P. Principles of data mining, The MIT Press, Cambridge, MA, 2001, pp. 5-6.*
- *Han J, Kamber M. Data Mining, Elsevier, Philadelphia, PA, 2006, pp 6-7.*
- *Hair JF, Black WC, Babin BJ, Anderson RE, Tatham RL. Multivariate data analysis, 6th Edition, Pearson Prentice Hall, Upper Saddle River, NJ, 2005, pp 561-564.*
- *Mikhaylovich VA, Pessirio BA. Labor Safety Standard for Diving Operations, Part II. Mortechinformreklama Publishing House, Moscow., 1992, p 60.*
- *Ozyigit T, Egi SM, Denoble PJ, Balestra C, Aydin S, Vann R, Marroni A. Decompression illness medically reported by hyperbaric treatment facilities: Cluster analysis of 1929 Cases. Aviat Space Environm Med 2010; 81(1):1-5.*
- *Vann RD, Denoble PJ, Uguccioni DM, Freiberger JJ, Perkins R, Reed W, Dovenbarger J, Caruso J. Report on Decompression Illness, Diving Fatalities and Project Dive Exploration: DAN's Annual Review. Divers Alert Network, Durham, NC, 2002.*


## Chapter 10


- *Boycott AE, Damant GCC, Haldane JS. The prevention of compressed air illness. J Hygiene 1908; 8(3): 342–443. In: Lang MA., Brubakk AO. (Eds) The Future of Diving: 100 Years of Haldane and Beyond. Smithsonian Scholarly*

*Press, Washington, D.C., 2009 (http://www.si.edu/dive/library_haldane.htm)*

- *Hagberg M, Ornhagen H. Incidence and risk factors for symptoms of decompression sickness among male and female dive masters and instructors – a retrospective cohort study. Undersea Hyperb Med 2003; 30(2):93-102.*
- *Longphre JM, Denoble PJ, Moon RE, Vann RD, Freiberger JJ. First aid normobaric oxygen for the treatment of recreational diving injuries. Undersea Hyperb Med. 2007; 34(1):43-9.*
- *Xu W, Liu W, Huang G, Zou Z, Cai Z, et al. Decompression Illness: clinical aspects of 5278 consecutive cases treated in a single hyperbaric unit. PLoS ONE 2012; 7(11): e50079. doi:10.1371/journal.pone.0050079.*
- *Blatteau JE, Gempp E, Constantin P, Louge P. Risk factors and clinical outcome in military divers with neurological decompression sickness: influence of time to recompression. Diving Hyperb Med. 2011; 41(3):129-34.*
- *Klingmann C, Praetorius M, Baumann I, Plinkert PK. Barotrauma and decompression illness of the inner ear: 46 cases during treatment and follow-up. Otol Neurotol. 2007; 28(4):447-54.*
- *Mitchell SJ, Doolette DJ, Wachholz CJ, Vann RD. Management of mild or marginal decompression illness in remote locations - Workshop Proceedings 2004; Divers Alert Network, Durham, NC, 2005.*
- *Burman F. Risk Assessment Guide for Recompression Chamber facilities. 2nd Edition. International ATMO, Inc. San Antonio, TX, 2011.*

**Chapter 11**

- *Balestra C, Lafère P, Germonpre P. Persistence of critical flicker fusion frequency impairment after a 33 msw scuba dive: evidence of prolonged nitrogen narcosis? Eur J Appl Physiol 2012; 112(12):4063-4068.*

- *Behnke AR, Thompson JC, Motley EP. Physiological effects from breathing air at four atmospheres pressure. Am J Physiol 1935; 112:554-558.*
- *Bennett PB, Cross AVC. Alterations in the fusion frequency of flicker correlated with electroencephalogram changes at increased partial pressure of nitrogen. J Physiol 1960; 151:28-29*
- *Fowler B, Ackles KN, Porlier G. Effects of inert gas narcosis on behavior--a critical review. Undersea Biomed Res 1985; 12(4):369-402*
- *Hemelryck W, Rozloznik M, Germonpré P, Balestra C, Lafère P. Functional comparison between critical flicker fusion frequency and simple cognitive tests in subjects breathing air or oxygen in normobaria. Diving Hyperb Med 2013; 43(3):138-42.*
- *Rostain JC, Lavoute C, Risso JJ, Vallee N, Weiss M. A review of recent neurochemical data on inert gas narcosis. Undersea Hyperb Med 2011; 38(1):49-59.*

## Chapter 12

- *Fock AW. Analysis of recreational closed-circuit rebreather deaths 1998-2010. Diving Hyperb Med. 2013;43(2):78-85.*
- *Mitchell SJ, Doolette DJ. Recreational technical diving Part 1: An introduction to technical diving methods and activities. Diving Hyperb Med. 2013;43(2):86-93.*
- *Doolette DJ, Mitchell SJ. Recreational technical diving Part 2: Decompression from deep technical dives. Diving Hyperb Med. 2013;43(2):96-104.*
- *Hemelryck W, Germonpré P, Papadopoulou V, Rozloznik M, Balestra C. Long term effects of recreational SCUBA*

*diving on higher cognitive function. Scand J Med Sci Sports. 2013 [Epub ahead of print].*
- *Balestra C, Germonpré P, Marroni A, Cronje FJ. PFO and the diver. Best Publishing Company, Flagstaff, AZ, 2007.*
- *Buzzacott PL. The epidemiology of injury in SCUBA diving. In: Caine D., Heggie T. (Eds): Epidemiology of Injury in Adventure and Extreme Sports, Karger AG – Medical and Scientific Publishers; Basel, Switzerland. 2012; pp. 57-79.*
- *Lang MA, Angelini, SA. The Future of Dive Computers. In: Lang MA, Brubakk AO. (Eds): The Future of Diving: 100 Years of Haldane and Beyond. Smithsonian Institution Scholarly Press, Washington, DC. 2009; pp 91-107.*
- *Piantadosi CA. The Biology of Human Survival. Life and Death in Extreme Environments. Oxford University Press; 2003.*

## Chapter 13

- *US Navy Diving Manual, Vol.2: Mixed gas diving, NAVSHIPS 0994-001-0910, US Navy Department, Washington, DC, 1973.*
- *Bornmann RC. Decompression schedule development for repetitive saturation-excursion helium-oxygen diving, US Navy Deep Submergence Systems Project Research Report 1-70, 1970.*
- *Workmann RD. Calculation of decompression schedules for nitrogen-oxygen and helium-oxygen dives. Navy Experimental Diving Unit Research Report 6-65, 1965.*
- *Summitt JK, Herron JM, Flynn ET. Repetitive excursion dives from saturated depths on helium-oxygen, Navy Experimental Diving Unit Research Report 2-70, 1970.*

- *Summitt JK, Alexander JM, Flynn ET, Herron JM. Repetitive excursion dives from saturated depths on helium-oxygen: Phase II - saturated depth 200ft. Navy Experimental Diving Unit Research Report 6-70, 1970.*
- *Spaur WH, Thalmann ED, Flynn T, Zumrick JL, Reedy TW, Ringleberg JM. Development of unlimited duration excursion tables and procedures for helium-oxygen saturation diving. Undersea Biomed Res. 1978;5:159–177*
- *Hempleman HV. The safety evaluation of saturation decompression tables. The Norwegian Petroleum Directorate, ISBN 82-7527-203.6, 1986.*
- *NORSOK Standards for Manned Underwater Operation. Norwegian Technology Standards Institution, Rev. 1. Oslo, Norway, 1999.*
- *Berghage TE. Decompression sickness during saturation dives. Undersea Biomed Res. 1976;3:387-398.*
- *Jacobsen C, Jacobsen JE, Petersen RE. et al. Decompression sickness from saturation diving: a case control study of some diving exposure characteristics. Undersea Hyperb Med. 1997;24:73-89.*
- *Buhlmann AA. Decompression theory, the Swiss practice. In: Bennett PB., Elliott DH. (Eds): The Physiology and Medicine of Diving and Compressed Air Work, 2nd Edition. Bailliere and Tindall, London, 1975; pp 348-365.*
- *Thalmann ED. Development of decompression algorithm for constant 0.7 ATA oxygen partial pressure in helium diving. Navy Experimental Diving Unit Research Report 1-85; 1986.*


### Food for Thought 1


- *McCormick TH, Rudin C, Madigan D. Bayesian hierarchical rule modeling for predicting medical conditions. Ann App Stat. 2012;6,652-68.*

- *Eftedal OS, Tjelmeland H, Brubakk AO. Validation of decompression procedures based on detection of venous gas bubbles: A Bayesian approach. Aviat Space Environ Med. 2007;78:94-9.*
- *Ozyigit T, Egi SM, Denoble P, Balestra C, Aydin S, Vann R, et al. Decompression illness medically reported by hyperbaric treatment facilities: cluster analysis of 1929 cases. Aviat Space Environ Med. 2010;81:3-7.*


**Food for Thought 2**


- *Brian, JE Jr. The Oxygen Window. 2001; available from from http://www.gap-software.com/staticfiles/Oxygen_Window.pdf (retrieved Jul 2014)*
- *Van Liew HD, Conkin J, Burkard ME (1993). "The oxygen window and decompression bubbles: estimates and significance". Aviation, Space, and Environmental Medicine 1993;64(9):859–65.*


**Food for Thought 3**


- *Papadopoulou V, Eckersley RJ, Balestra C, Karapantsios TD, Tang MX. A critical review of physiological bubble formation in hyperbaric decompression. Adv Colloid Interface Sci. 2013;191-192:22-30.*
- *Papadopoulou V, Tang M-X, Balestra C, Eckersley RJ, Karapantsios TD. Circulatory bubble dynamics: From physical to biological aspects. Adv Colloid Interface Sci. 2014; 206:239-249*
- *Dervay JP, Powell MR, Butler B, Fife CE. The effect of exercise and rest duration on the generation of venous gas bubbles at altitude. Aviat Space Environ Med.. 2002;73:22-7.*

- *Wisloff U, Brubakk AO. Aerobic endurance training reduces bubble formation and increases survival in rats exposed to hyperbaric pressure. J Physiol. 2001;537:607-11.*
- *Wisloff U, Richardson RS, Brubakk AO. Exercise and nitric oxide prevent bubble formation: a novel approach to the prevention of decompression sickness? J Physiol. 2004;555:825-9.*
- *Carturan D, Boussuges A, Burnet H, Fondarai J, Vanuxem P, Gardette B. Circulating venous bubbles in recreational diving: relationships with age, weight, maximal oxygen uptake and body fat percentage. Int J Sports Med. 1999;20:410-4.*
- *Dujic Z, Valic Z, Brubakk AO. Beneficial role of exercise on scuba diving. Exercise Sport Sci Rev. 2008;36:38-42.*
- *Blatteau JE, Boussuges A, Gempp E, Pontier JM, Castagna O, Robinet C, et al. Haemodynamic changes induced by submaximal exercise before a dive and its consequences on bubble formation. Br J Sports Med. 2007;41:375-9.*
- *Blatteau JE, Gempp E, Galland FM, Pontier JM, Sainty JM, Robinet C. Aerobic exercise 2 hours before a dive to 30 msw decreases bubble formation after decompression. Aviat Space Environ Med. 2005;76:666-9.*
- *Castagna O, Brisswalter J, Vallee N, Blatteau JE. Endurance exercise immediately before sea diving reduces bubble formation in scuba divers. Eur J Appl Physiol. 2011;111:1047-54.*
- *Dujic Z, Palada I, Valic Z, Duplancic D, Obad A, Wisloff U, et al. Exogenous nitric oxide and bubble formation in divers. Med Sci Sports Exerc. 2006;38:1432-5.*
- *Wisloff U, Richardson RS, Brubakk AO. NOS inhibition increases bubble formation and reduces survival in sedentary but not exercised rats. J Physiol. 2003;546:577-82.*

- *Germonpré P, Pontier JM, Gempp E, Blatteau JE, Deneweth S, Lafere P, et al. Pre-dive vibration effect on bubble formation after a 30-m dive requiring a decompression stop. Aviat Space Environ Med.. 2009;80:1044-8.*
- *Hyldegaard O, Madsen J. Effect of air, heliox, and oxygen breathing on air bubbles in aqueous tissues in the rat. Undersea Hyperb Med 1994;21:413-24.*
- *Hyldegaard O, Moller M, Madsen J. Effect of He-O2, O2, and N2O-O2 breathing on injected bubbles in spinal white matter. Undersea Biomed Res. 1991;18:361-71.*
- *Hyldegaard O, Madsen J. Influence of heliox, oxygen, and N2O-O2 breathing on N2 bubbles in adipose tissue. Undersea Biomed Res. 1989;16:185-93.*


**Food for Thought 4**


- *Hills BA. A hydrophobic oligolamellar lining to the vascular lumen in some organs. Undersea Biomed Res 1992; 19:107-120.*
- *Arieli R, Marmur A. Dynamics of gas micronuclei formed on a flat hydrophobic surface, the predecessors of decompression bubbles. Resp Physiol Neurobiol 2013; 185:647-652.*
- *Arieli R, Marmur A. Ex vivo bubble production from ovine large blood vessels: Size on detachment and evidence of "active spots". Resp Physiol Neurobiol 2014; 200:110-117.*
- *Philp RB, Inwood MJ, Warren BA. Interactions between gas bubbles and components of the blood: implications in decompression sickness. Aerospace Med 1972; 43:946-953.*
- *Vadasz Z, Haj T, Kessel A, Toubi E. Age-related autoimmunity. BMC Med 2013; 11:94.*

- *Arieli R. Was the appearance of surfactants in air breathing vertebrates ultimately the cause of decompression sickness and autoimmune disease ? Resp Physiol Neurobiol. Epub 2014 Nov 18.*
- *Germonpré P, Pontier JM, Gempp E, Blatteau JE, Deneweth S, Lafere P, Marroni A, Balestra C. Pre-dive vibration effect on bubble formation after a 30m dive requiring a decompression stop. Aviat Space Environ Med 2009; 80: 1044-1048.*
- *Castagna O, Gempp E, Blatteau JE. Pre-dive normobaric oxygen reduces bubble formation in scuba divers. Eur J Appl Physiol 2009; 106:167-172.*
- *Blatteau JE, Gempp E, Balestra C, Mets T, Germonpré P. Predive sauna and venous gas bubbles upon decompression from 400kPa. Aviat Space Environm Med 2008; 79:1100-1105.*
- *Madden D, Thom SR, Yang M, Bhopale VM, Ljubkovic M, Dujic Z.High intensity cycling before SCUBA diving reduces post-decompression microparticle production and neutrophil activation. Eur J Appl Physiol. 2014; 114:1955-61*


## Food for Thought 5


- *Calzia E, Asfar P, Hauser B, Matejovic M, Balestra C, Radermacher P, et al. Hyperoxia may be beneficial. Crit Care Med. 2010;38:S559-68.*
- *Meyhoff CS, Staehr AK, Rasmussen LS. Rational use of oxygen in medical disease and anesthesia. Curr Op in Anesthesiology. 2012;25:363-70.*
- *Asfar P, Calzia E, Huber-Lang M, Ignatius A, Radermacher P. Hyperoxia during septic shock - Dr. Jekyll or Mr. Hyde? Shock. 2012;37:122-3.*

- *Balestra C, Germonpre P. Hypoxia, a multifaceted phenomenon: the example of the "Normobaric Oxygen Paradox". Eur J Appl Physiol. 2012;112:4173-4175*


**Food for Thought 6**


- *Cyr A, Cyr LO, Cyr C. Acquired growth hormone deficiency and hypo-gonadotropic hypogonadism in a subject with repeated head trauma, or: Tintin goes to the neurologist. CMAJ. 2004;171:1433-4.*
- *Upper D. The unsuccessful self-treatment of a case of "writer's block". Journal of Applied Behavior Analysis. 1974;7: 497.*
- *Didden R, Sigafood J, O'Reilly M, Sturmey P. A multisite cross-cultural replication of Upper's (1974) unsuccessful self-treatment of writer's block. Journal of Applied Behavior Analysis. 2007;40:773.*
- *Alterhaug B. Creativity and improvisation as phenomena and acting potential in different contexts. In: Lang M, Editor. The future of diving: 100 years of Haldane and beyond. Washington DC: Smithsonian Scholarly Press; 2009. p. 161-70. Available at http://archive.rubicon-foundation.org/xmlui/handle/123456789/9242.*

Printed in the USA
CPSIA information can be obtained
at www.ICGtesting.com
LVHW011240070424
776682LV00009B/925